Christmas, 1983

To Bea

From your slap-dash but devoted friend

Mary

THE ORIENTAL GOURMET

THE ORIENTAL GOURMET

GREAT RECIPES OF JAPAN AND SOUTHEAST ASIA

SAUL KRIEG

CHELSEA HOUSE
NEW YORK, LONDON
1982

Printed and bound in the United States of America

ISBN: 0-87754-359-3
LC: 82-70289

Chelsea House Publishers
Harold Steinberg, Chairman & Publisher
Andrew E. Norman, President
Susan Lusk, Vice President
A Division of Chelsea House Educational Communications, Inc.
133 Christopher St., New York 10014

Contents

Introduction

The foods of Japan and Southeast Asia have a national and ethnic flavor all their own, and the recipes in this book will enable you to capture that flavor for your own dinners and parties. They are all delicious, different and easy to prepare. The major focus is on Japan, with a sampling of savory dishes from Burma, China, Hong Kong, Indonesia and Thailand. You will find unfamiliar terms or ingredients defined in the glossary.

The Joy of Japanese Cooking

Japanese cuisine is both an adventure in good taste and an artistic achievement, a joyful experience to prepare as well as to eat. The chefs of Japan are not only masters of fine cooking but also of the decorative arts that make their creations so unique, dramatic and romantic.

A typical Japanese dinner includes fish and shellfish, vegetables and delicate soups as well as more hearty fare. Portions are small to allow for several courses of meats and vegetables accompanied by piquant sauces. As an honor to his guests, the host attends to the beverages and fills or refills their glasses. This custom is also observed in most Japanese restaurants.

The restaurants of Japan range from noodle palaces and tempura houses to small inns serving authentic regional specialties. The restaurants in Tokyo and Osaka are marvels of great cooking in three different styles: Oriental, Western (even French) and Japanese. Away from the big cities, the dishes are often challenging but always excellent.

In recent years the unusual and flavorful cuisine of Japan and the Orient has made an increasing number of converts throughout the United States. More and more Japanese restaurants have been opening in major cities around the nation, and Japanese steakhouses and tempura restaurants have become especially popular. As the guests sit at tables with flat, open stoves in front of them, talented chefs prepare shrimp, steaks, vegetables and other delicacies right before their eyes. The chefs put on an exciting show, dramatically highlighted by flashing knives, while kimono-clad waitresses serve soups and sauces and the teas of Japan.

Japanese Beverages: The Kirin Mystique

Nowadays in Japan the consumption of beer far exceeds that of sake, the rice wine usually thought of as Japan's national drink (actually sake is not a wine but a true brew, fermented like beer). Beer consumption accounts for 67% of Japan's alcoholic intake, and sake for 23.5%. Whiskey is another popular alcoholic beverage, but beer is now the national drink of Japan. And the best-selling beer in Japan is Kirin, the favorite beverage of the Japanese people.

The history of Kirin beer can be traced back to the opening of Japan to world trade and commerce. In 1853 Commodore Matthew C. Perry of the United States Navy visited Japan, and the next year he secured ratification of a treaty opening Japan to trade with the West. A few years later Japan entered the commercial mainstream and began developing into the highly industrialized modern nation it is today.

The first brewery in Japan, the Spring Valley Brewery in Yokohama, was established by an American in 1869, fifteen years after Commodore Perry's visit. Production was small, but the foreigners who resided in the locality enjoyed the brew.

The American brewer sold his company to the Japan Brewing Company in 1888, and the Japanese firm changed the brand name and improved the quality of the beer significantly. The new name appeared on the first bottle along with a symbol of the mythical creature from which it came and which has been the trademark of the beer ever since. The Kirin, according to ancient Chinese legend, foretold the birth of a saint and is regarded as a symbol of happiness and good fortune. Today the Kirin still represents the better things in life, such as Kirin beer.

Kirin is an elegant premium lager beer, one of the finest in the world. It is made from the best malted barley, hops, yeast, water and rice, double-fermented, matured in vats and double-filtered. The Japanese love Kirin and serve it at every opportunity, with luncheons and dinners, and even as an after-dinner drink.

Kirin is also very popular in the United States, where it had its introduction in Chinese, Asian and Japanese restaurants. Now it is available in most fine restaurants, and in supermarkets, groceries, specialty shops and delis.

A "Cook's Tour" of Japan

Japan is an archipelago consisting of four main islands and more than 1,000 smaller islands, a scenic wonderland of tailored landscapes, beautiful trees and plants, mountains and oceans, valleys and plains, islets and dramatic coastlines. In total area it is not quite as large as California and about half the size of France. As of 1980, its population was estimated at 116,780,000.

Tokyo, the capital city of Japan, lies on the main island of Honshu. West of Tokyo are the other major cities: Yokohama, Nagoya, Kyoto, Osaka and Kobe. Most of Japan's population, money, industry, farmland, history, beauty, recreation, temples and art are concentrated in this region, which is a continuous blend of urbanization and tradition, a complete modern composite. New shops, restaurants, cafés and amusement parks as well as all types of theaters abound in the cities. The side streets are alive and buzzing with activity. In strong contrast to this urban Japan are its villages and farms. Arable land is scarce in Japan, and most of it is devoted to raising crops. Rice is an important staple.

For all their independent thinking and industrial innovation, the Japanese are also great borrowers. Japan is only 150 miles from China and has accepted much in the way of Chinese culture—art, legends, mythology, religion—though in an inimitably Japanese way. Now, with the addition of Western-style politics and technology, Japan is an exotic mixture of old and new, modern and traditional.

The people of Japan have their own code of ethics and behavior. They are very courteous and helpful to visitors, though their teachings, way of life and way of thinking are very different from those of Westerners. For example, they sometimes seem almost evasive in response to questions, but that is a Western misinterpretation of their extreme politeness and reticence. With growing numbers of Europeans and Americans visiting Japan, however, the Japanese have become more accustomed to foreign ways. They are now bolder, more outgoing and less inhibited in their dealings with Western tourists. And their hotels and inns are wonderful, offering fine accommodations in both Western and native style.

All in all, Japan is a marvelous place to visit. But if you can't make the trip this year, that's all right. You can have almost as much fun by staying home and sampling the variety and flavor of this unique land and its neighbors in your own kitchen and dining room.

1
Appetizers

The appetizers of Japan and Southeast Asia make perfect companion snacks to enjoy with Kirin beer, served in chilled, frosted glasses. Kirin is a mellow beer and goes perfectly with these piquant, spicy, aromatic appetizers. The recipes in this chapter are designed both to complement the beer and to whet the appetite for the meal to come.

For your next dinner party, serve some of these appetizers with drinks or as your first course. You might also consider serving a selection of them as a unique luncheon for your bridge or club guests or even as a light Sunday meal. Whatever the occasion, these appetizers are tasty and simple to make, and they will win you applause for your originality and creative hosting.

PORK MEATBALLS ON BAMBOO STICKS

1½ lbs. lean ground pork
1 onion, finely chopped
½ Tbs. ginger juice
¼ cup sifted flour
1 slice of white bread, trimmed and soaked in lukewarm water
¼ cup soy sauce
1 tsp. sugar
1 Tbs. sweet sherry
1 Tbs. water
Chopped flat parsley for garnish

Thoroughly mix the ground pork with the onion, ginger juice and flour. Squeeze moisture out of bread and work bread into pork mixture until smooth. Form into meatballs the size of ping-pong balls.

In a saucepan combine the soy sauce, sugar, sherry and water. Stir while bringing to a boil, then lower heat to a simmer. Add meatballs and cook until liquid is reduced by half and meat is done, 12-15 minutes. Thread meatballs onto bamboo sticks and garnish with chopped parsley.

Serves 4-6

OYSTERS ON THE HALF SHELL IN LEMON SAUCE

12 fresh oysters
3 scallions (whites and 2″ of greens) for garnish

Lemon Sauce:
2 Tbs. grated white radish
1 tsp. soy sauce
⅛ tsp. ground white pepper
2 Tbs. white wine vinegar
2 Tbs. freshly squeezed lemon juice
½ tsp. finely grated lemon peel

Wash and sever oysters, remove from shells, and reserve shells. Finely mince scallions and reserve.

To prepare lemon sauce, combine all the ingredients in a large bowl and mix well. Add oysters and drench thoroughly in sauce.

Return oysters to their shells with a large spoon and arrange them on a platter, handling shells gently so that sauce does not spill. Sprinkle with scallions and serve.

Serves 4-6

STEAMED CHICKEN DUMPLINGS WITH SPECIAL DIP-SAUCE

1 cup raw rice,
  soaked in water overnight
2 cups finely chopped chicken
¼ cup minced onion
½ cup chopped fresh mushrooms
2 Tbs. sugar
3 Tbs. cornstarch
1 Tbs. sherry
Scant ¼ cup soy sauce

Dip-Sauce:
1 clove garlic, finely minced
½ cup soy sauce
½ tsp. ginger juice

Drain the rice and spread on a large board.

Combine chicken with onions, mushrooms and sugar, and blend in cornstarch. Add sherry and soy sauce. Mix thoroughly and form into small balls.

Roll the chicken balls in the rice, making sure each ball is well coated. Place balls in a steamer and steam for 20 minutes.

To make dip-sauce, beat the ingredients together with a wooden spoon until well blended.

Serve dumplings in a large bowl, accompanied by sauce for dipping.

Serves 6-8

STUFFED CUCUMBER RINGS WITH CRABMEAT FILLING

4 medium-size cucumbers
1 7-oz. can of crabmeat
2 Tbs. white wine vinegar
1 Tbs. dashi or chicken broth
1½ tsp. sugar
¼ tsp. salt
1 tsp. soy sauce
Yolks of 2 hard-boiled eggs for garnish

Peel cucumbers and cut into slices ½″ thick. Cut out the seedy center portion of each cucumber slice to make rings.

Drain crabmeat and chop coarsely. Combine crabmeat with vinegar, broth, sugar, salt and soy sauce, mixing thoroughly. Press the crabmeat filling into the cucumber rings and place in the refrigerator to chill through. Sprinkle with a garnish of chopped egg yolk and serve.

Serves 6-8

HOT PUMPKIN WITH PEANUT BUTTER SAUCE

½ small pumpkin
¼ cup cornstarch
Vegetable oil for frying

Peanut Butter Sauce:
2 heaping Tbs. peanut butter
1 Tbs. miso
1 Tbs. white wine vinegar

Remove seeds from pumpkin and cut into slices ¼″ thick. Do not peel. Dredge pumpkin slices in cornstarch and fry in hot oil until golden on both sides, 6-8 minutes per side. Remove to paper toweling to drain.

To prepare the sauce, mix peanut butter with miso and vinegar until smooth. Put the sauce in small dishes for each person and serve with pumpkin slices.

Serves 4

GRILLED SHRIMP AND SCALLOPS ON SKEWERS

8 medium-size shrimp, shelled and cleaned, with tails
8 scallops
4 scallion whites, cut in half lengthwise
8 mushrooms
8 small white pearl onions

Marinade:
½ cup soy sauce
1 Tbs. sherry
3 Tbs. sake
1 Tbs. lemon juice
Dash of pepper

Prepare marinade first. Combine ingredients in a saucepan, bring to a boil and remove from heat.

Add shrimp and scallops and marinate for ½ hour, turning a few times. Drain and reserve marinade for basting.

Thread the seafood and vegetables onto skewers, alternating shrimp, scallion, mushroom, scallop and onion, one skewer per person. Grill over a high flame for about 5 minutes on each side or until brown, brushing frequently with marinade.

Remove skewers to a lettuce bed on a serving platter. Serve with pepper and the remaining marinade for dipping.

Serves 4

MIXED BATTERED GRILL

1 lb. chicken wings
¾ lb. very lean beef (chuck, rump or round), thinly sliced
¾ lb. chicken livers
1 large green pepper, sliced in strips
Vegetable oil for frying

Batter:
1½ cups flour
¼ tsp. salt
2 dashes ground black pepper
1 egg, separated
½ cup Kirin beer

Sauce:
2 Tbs. soy sauce
1 Tbs. sweet sherry
1 Tbs. sake
1 Tbs. sugar
⅛ tsp. ground Japanese pepper

Prepare batter first. Sift together flour, salt and pepper. Combine with lightly beaten egg yolk and slowly stir in the beer. Add more sifted flour if necessary. Beat egg white until stiff and fold into batter. Batter should be smooth and slightly thickened.

Heat oil in a deep pot for frying. Dip chicken wings into batter and fry until golden brown all over. Dip beef slices into batter and fry until batter is lightly browned, 2–3 minutes. Repeat same procedure for chicken livers and pepper slices. Remove meats and pepper slices to paper toweling to drain, then place on a heated platter while you make the sauce.

Combine all the sauce ingredients in a saucepan and bring to a boil, stirring all the time. Remove from heat and pour into a sauce bowl.

Serve the Mixed Battered Grill with chopsticks, small forks or party toothpicks, using the sauce as a dip.

Serves 8-10

BROILED CHICKEN LIVERS ON SMALL SKEWERS

¾ lb. chicken livers
6 large scallions
3 turns of ground black pepper for garnish

Glazing Sauce:
¼ cup soy sauce
2 Tbs. sweet wine
1 Tbs. sake
1 Tbs. honey
1 heaping tsp. sugar

Wash and drain chicken livers and cut in half. Chop scallion greens and reserve for garnish. Thread chicken liver halves and scallion whites alternately on small steel skewers. Set aside.

To prepare glazing sauce, combine ingredients in a saucepan over moderate heat and stir until mixture comes to a boil. Remove from heat.

Broil skewered livers and scallions for about 1½ minutes, turning frequently. Remove, saturate thoroughly with glazing sauce, and return to broiler for an additional ½ minute, until sauce glazes over.

Sprinkle with ground black pepper and chopped scallion greens.

Serves 4-6

PARTY MUSHROOMS WITH LEMON JUICE

½ lb. fresh mushrooms
8 large dried black mushrooms
½ cup dashi or chicken broth
3 Tbs. soy sauce
3 Tbs. dry sherry
Freshly squeezed juice of ½ lemon

Wash the fresh mushrooms. Soak the dried mushrooms in water, drain and pat dry. Cut mushrooms into thin slices, leaving ½″ of stem.

In a saucepan stir together the broth, soy sauce and sherry, and heat to just under a boil. Add mushrooms and continue stirring for 3 minutes.

Strain the sauce into a bowl. Put the mushrooms in a separate bowl and sprinkle with lemon juice. Serve with sauce.

Serves 6-8

ASPARAGUS WITH BEAN PASTE

1 dozen fresh asparagus
½ tsp. salt
1 Tbs. soy sauce
2 Tbs. miso

Wash asparagus and trim off hard ends. Cook them in salted boiling water, ¾ covered, until tender.

Arrange asparagus on a board and fan them so they will cool rapidly and stay green. Place asparagus on a platter and pour soy sauce over them. Melt the miso in a small saucepan and spread it over the asparagus.

Serves 4-6

SHRIMP-STUFFED DEEP-FRIED MUSHROOM CAPS WITH SAUCE

12 large fresh mushrooms
¼ lb. shrimp,
  shelled and cleaned
¼ cup cornstarch
1/3 cup wondra flour
½ cup water
Vegetable oil for frying

Sauce:
½ cup clear chicken broth
1 Tbs. sweet wine
3 Tbs. soy sauce
1/3 cup grated white radish

Wash mushrooms, remove stems and pat caps dry. Using an electric food processor, turn the shrimp into a smooth paste. Coat each mushroom cavity with a little cornstarch and stuff with the shrimp paste.

In a bowl mix the remaining cornstarch with the flour and water to form a batter. Heat the oil in a deep skillet until hot, then lower to a light simmer. Dip the mushroom caps in the batter and deep-fry until golden brown.

To prepare sauce, mix the ingredients in a saucepan and bring to a boil, stirring all the time. Remove from heat and pour into small dipping bowls. Serve with fried mushroom caps.

Serves 4

SALMON CAVIAR IN KUMQUAT SHELLS

8 kumquats
8 oz. salmon caviar
1 scallion, thinly sliced,
  for garnish

Cut stems and tops off the kumquats. Remove pulp and discard. Fill kumquats with caviar and garnish the tops with scallions.

Serves 4

FISH PANCAKES

¼ cup vegetable oil
1 tsp. ground chili pepper
2 onions, minced
½ tsp. grated lemon rind
2 cloves garlic, finely minced
1 tsp. salt
1 lb. ground fillet of sole
1 Tbs. flour (more if needed)
2 tomatoes, minced

Heat half the oil in a heavy skillet. Add the chili peppers, onions, lemon rind, garlic and salt, and cook at moderate heat for 8 minutes, stirring continually.

Strain off the oil, remove ingredients to a bowl and allow to cool. Add the ground fish and mix thoroughly. Form the mixture into balls about 2" in diameter and sprinkle with flour.

Heat the balance of the vegetable oil in the skillet. Add fish balls and brown all over. Add tomatoes and cook for 15 minutes longer. Serve with rice or noodles.

Serves 2-4

GINGERED EGGS

4 hard-boiled eggs
4 Tbs. peanut oil
2 onions, minced
1/3 tsp. chopped ginger
½ tsp. salt
¾ tsp. paprika
¾ cup tomato puree
¾ cup water
2 tsp. soy sauce

Cut the hard-boiled eggs in half lengthwise. Heat the oil and saute the onions and ginger until onions start to turn color. Stir in salt and paprika.

Add tomato puree and water and bring to a boil. Stir in soy sauce, add eggs and cook at a simmer until egg whites are colored, about 3 minutes. Serve warm.

Serves 6-8

CURRIED SHRIMP

1 Tbs. soy sauce
1/3 tsp. turmeric
⅛ tsp. curry powder
¾ tsp. paprika
1 lb. shrimp, shelled and cleaned

3 Tbs. vegetable oil
3 onions, minced
1 clove garlic, minced
1/3 tsp. ground ginger
¾ cup tomato puree
½ cup water

Make a marinade by combining the soy sauce, turmeric, curry powder and paprika in a large bowl. Add shrimp and allow to marinate for 1 hour or longer.

Heat the oil and sauté the onions, garlic and ginger for 3 minutes. Stir the marinated shrimp, then add them to the onion mixture with a slotted spoon, along with several Tbs. of the marinade. Stir.

Cook at a simmer for 3 minutes. Add tomato puree and water, continuing to simmer until the mixture is heated through. Serve over hot rice.

Serves 4-6

FILLED WONTONS

Wrappers:
2 cups flour
½ tsp. salt
½ cup cold water
1 egg, lightly beaten

Filling:
2½ Tbs. peanut oil
¼ lb. ground pork
½ lb. shrimp, shelled, cleaned and chopped
3 tsp. soy sauce
1 tsp. cream sherry
4 water chestnuts, chopped
1 scallion, chopped
¾ tsp. cornstarch mixed with ¾ tsp. water
1 cup peanut oil for frying

To make the wrappers, sift together flour and salt, make a well in the flour, and pour into it the cold water and beaten egg. Knead into a soft ball with your hands, remove to a floured board, and continue kneading until smooth, about 3–4 minutes.

Divide the dough into 4 balls. Roll each ball out onto a floured board until it is about 1/8″ thick. Cut into 3½″ squares to make individual wrappers.

To make the filling, heat the 2½ Tbs. peanut oil in a wok or skillet. Stir-fry the pork for 2 minutes, then add the shrimp, soy sauce, sherry, water chestnuts and scallions and stir-fry for 2 minutes more. Add the cornstarch and water, stirring until filling thickens. Remove filling to a bowl and allow to cool.

Place 1½ tsp. of the filling in the middle of each wrapper. Wet the edges of the wrapper dough with your fingers. Bring one corner of the wrapper over the filling to the opposite corner but not quite to the edge, fold the two corners to overlap, and pinch them together with moistened fingers. Leave the other two corners as they are.

The filled wontons are now ready to be deep-fried in the cup of peanut oil. They can also be cooked in soup.

Makes 24 or more wontons

AROMATIC SPARERIBS

2–3 lbs. spareribs

Sauce, Step 1:
2 Tbs. soy sauce
2 Tbs. dry sherry
2 Tbs. sugar
1 tsp. Chinese spices
2 Tbs. hoisin sauce
1½ cups boiling water

Sauce, Step 2:
3 Tbs. soy sauce
3 Tbs. dry sherry
4 Tbs. oil
2 cloves garlic, crushed
3 Tbs. honey

Cut each sparerib in half.

In a saucepan combine all the Step 1 sauce ingredients except the boiling water, heat and stir until the mixture boils. Remove from heat and add spareribs. Marinate spareribs for 20 minutes.

Add the boiling water to the saucepan, stir and return to a boil. Lower heat to a simmer, cover saucepan, and cook for 30 minutes, turning the ribs several times. Drain ¼ cup of sauce into a bowl and reserve the rest.

Mix the ¼ cup of sauce with the soy sauce in Step 2. Stir in the sherry and set aside.

Heat the oil in a wok or heavy skillet, add the garlic and honey, then slowly add the ¼ cup sauce, stirring until the mixture bubbles. Add the ribs and cook for an additional 5 minutes. Keep turning and coating the ribs all over with the sauce. Remove ribs to a bowl and serve at once, accompanied by reserved sauce from Step 1.

Serves 10–12

CHINESE WINGS

12 chicken wings

¼ cup vegetable oil for frying

Marinade:

¼ cup soy sauce
¼ cup honey
½ cup hoisin sauce
1 cup boiling water

Batter:

2 Tbs. flour
2 Tbs. cornstarch
1 tsp. salt
1 egg, lightly beaten
1½ Tbs. water

Prepare the marinade first. Combine the soy sauce, honey and hoisin sauce in a saucepan and mix well. Stir until just under a boil, add the cup of boiling water, stir again and cover the saucepan. Cook at a simmer for 10 minutes, stirring once during this time. Remove from heat and marinate the chicken wings for 1 hour, turning several times during marination.

To make the batter, mix the flour, cornstarch and salt, blend in the egg and water, and stir. Heat the oil in a wok or heavy skillet, dip the wings in batter, and fry until golden brown all over, about 10 minutes. Drain and serve hot.

Serves 6

ORIENTAL BLACK MUSHROOMS

1 cup water
18 dried black mushrooms
4 Tbs. vegetable oil
2 Tbs. soy sauce
1 Tbs. honey
1 Tbs. sesame oil

Boil the water, remove from heat, and soak the dried mushrooms for 30 minutes, covered. Squeeze mushrooms dry and reserve water.

Heat the vegetable oil in a saucepan, add mushrooms, and stir over brisk heat for 3 minutes. Add soy sauce and honey. Stir.

Add ½ cup of the reserved mushroom water and bring to a boil. Lower heat and simmer for 30 minutes. Add sesame oil and stir. Serve hot or cold.

Serves 4-6

PORK IN SWEET SAUCE

½ cup hoisin sauce
1 Tbs. Chinese spices
2 garlic cloves, crushed
2 lbs. boneless loin of pork

Sauce:
4 Tbs. soy sauce
5 slices of ginger
1 tsp. Chinese duck sauce
2 scallions, whites halved, greens chopped
2 cups boiling water

Whip together the hoisin sauce, Chinese spices and garlic to make a marinade. Add the pork loin and turn to soak all over. Cover the bowl with plastic wrap and allow meat to marinate in the refrigerator for at least 4 hours. Turn twice during marination.

To prepare the sauce, combine the soy sauce, ginger slices, duck sauce and scallions, add the boiling water and stir. Bring to a boil, stir, and add the loin of pork. Cover and simmer for 1 hour until pork is tender. Turn once during cooking.

When pork is tender, remove from heat and let it soak in the sauce for 20 minutes. Remove pork to a bowl and allow to chill. Slice pork thinly, reheat the sauce, and serve it over the pork or on the side.

Serves 10-12

SHRIMP BALLS

- 1¼ lbs. shrimp, shelled, cleaned and chopped
- 4 water chestnuts, minced
- 2 scallion whites, shredded and chopped
- 2 Tbs. soy sauce
- 1 egg white, beaten foamy
- 1 Tbs. minced ginger
- 5 tsp. water
- ¼ cup cornstarch
- 1 Tbs. sesame oil
- 2 cups vegetable oil for frying

Mince the chopped shrimp, but do not make it pasty. Place in a bowl, add water chestnuts, scallions and soy sauce, and blend thoroughly. Add the foamy egg white and mix until smooth.

In a separate bowl, crush the minced ginger and add the water. Strain off the ginger and mix the water and cornstarch thoroughly. Add to the shrimp mixture and mix until fluffy.

Using the sesame oil to oil your hands, form about 20 shrimp balls. Heat the cooking oil in a wok or skillet and fry the shrimp balls in the hot oil, browning until crisp, about 5 minutes. Remove the finished shrimp balls to a heated platter and serve hot to avoid shrinking. Do not allow shrimp balls to cool.

Serves 6-8

CHICKEN LIVERS IN BACON ROLLS

20 chicken livers
¼ tsp. sliced ginger
1 scallion, sliced
6 water chestnuts
  cut into ⅛″ slices
10 slices of raw bacon,
  cut in half
1 Tbs. flour mixed with
  1 Tbs. cornstarch
Vegetable oil for frying

Marinade:
1 Tbs. soy sauce
1 Tbs. sugar
1 tsp. crushed ginger
1 Tbs. hoisin sauce

Prepare the marinade first by mixing all the ingredients thoroughly. Marinate the chicken livers for 10 minutes, remove from marinade and cut in half.

Put livers in a saucepan with the sliced ginger and scallions, cover with boiling water and simmer for 5 minutes. Remove livers and pat dry with paper towels.

Place a slice of water chestnut between 2 liver halves and wrap a slice of bacon around. Put the bacon rolls in a metal dish or the top of a double boiler and steam over a high flame for 3 minutes on each side, or until a coating forms on the livers. Allow rolls to cool, then refrigerate for ½ hour.

Return rolls to room temperature. Dredge them in the flour-cornstarch mixture and fry in hot oil for 5 minutes, until very crisp, turning a few times. Drain and serve hot.

Serves 8–10

SPRING ROLLS

- 2 Tbs. peanut oil
- ½ lb. ground pork
- ½ cup raw shrimp, shelled, cleaned and minced
- 2/3 cup shredded Chinese cabbage
- ½ cup minced water chestnuts
- 1 onion, chopped
- 1 tsp. soy sauce
- Salt and pepper to taste
- 1 1-lb. package of egg-roll skins
- 1 egg white, stiffly beaten
- 2 cups peanut oil for frying

Heat the 2 Tbs. peanut oil in a skillet, add ground pork and stir until lightly browned. Add the shrimp and fry for 3 minutes, stirring gently. Remove from heat to cool, and drain off the oil.

Mix together the cabbage, water chestnuts, onion, soy sauce, salt and pepper. Add pork and shrimp mixture and stir well.

Lay the egg-roll skins out on a board and put 2 large spoonfuls of the filling mixture in the center of each. Fold one of the long sides of the skin over the mixture, then fold the two short sides, and finally fold over the other long side. Seal the rolls by brushing them with the egg white.

Heat the 2 cups of peanut oil in a skillet and deep-fry the spring rolls until stiff and golden. Drain on paper toweling and serve hot with Chinese mustard and duck sauce.

Serves 4-6

SHRIMP DUMPLINGS

Dough:
2 cups flour
¼ tsp. salt
¾ cup ice water

Filling:
1 lb. shrimp, shelled, cleaned and cut in half
½ lb. ground pork
1 scallion (white and 2″ of green), chopped
1½ tsp. soy sauce
1/3 tsp. sesame oil
Salt and pepper to taste

To make the dough, sift flour and salt into a mixing bowl, add the water, and blend with your hands until the mixture is stiff. Knead and punch dough until smooth. Cover bowl with a damp towel and allow to stand ½ hour before filling.

To make the filling, thoroughly combine all the ingredients.

Roll the dumpling dough into balls about 2½″ in diameter. Press a cavity into the center of each ball, fill and pinch together at the top.

Place dumplings on a greased pan or in the top of a double boiler. Steam over boiling water for 12–15 minutes, covered. Serve very hot with duck sauce and Chinese mustard.

Makes about 24 large dumplings

BEEF PASTIES

Dough:
2½ cups all-purpose flour
1 egg, lightly beaten
1 cup water

Filling:
2 Tbs. peanut oil
1 lb. ground beef
4 scallion whites, thinly sliced
½ cup shredded Chinese cabbage
1 tsp. soy sauce
1 tsp. salt
Vegetable oil for frying
1/3 cup hot dashi or beef broth

To make the dough, combine the flour with the egg and enough water to make a soft dough. Knead dough gently on a floured board, roll thin and cut into a dozen or so 3″ rounds.

To make the filling, heat the 2 Tbs. peanut oil, add beef and fry for 10 minutes. Add scallions and cabbage and fry for 2 minutes more. Allow to cool and stir in soy sauce and salt.

Place a small amount of filling in the center of each dough round. Dampen dough edges with wet fingers, fold over and press tightly to seal.

Heat the frying oil in a wok or saucepan and fry the pasties until golden, turning once. Add hot broth, cover and simmer for 6 minutes. Remove pasties and drain.

Makes about 12 pasties

EGG ROLLS

Wrappers:

1¾ cups flour
1 Tbs. cornstarch
½ tsp. salt
1 egg, lightly beaten
¾ cup ice water

Filling:

½ lb. bean sprouts
½ lb. shrimp, shelled and cleaned
½ lb. boneless pork
6 Tbs. peanut oil
2 cups chopped celery
½ cup thinly sliced fresh mushrooms
2 scallions (whites and 2″ of greens), chopped
1 Tbs. soy sauce
1 Tbs. dry sherry
1 tsp. salt
½ tsp. sugar
1 Tbs. cornstarch dissolved in 2 Tbs. chicken broth
1 egg white, stiffly beaten, for sealing
Peanut oil for frying

To make the wrappers, sift the flour, cornstarch and salt into a large bowl. Stir in the beaten egg, then add the water gradually, mixing all the time. Knead the dough with your hands to make it elastic, and continue kneading until smooth, about 5-6 minutes. Cover the bowl with a dampened cloth and set aside for at least ½ hour.

Cut the dough into 4 parts, lightly flour a board, and roll out each dough ball until paper-thin. With a sharp knife, cut dough into 6″ squares. Set wrappers aside until ready to fill.

To make the filling, rinse the bean sprouts and soak them in water for 15 minutes, discarding the husks, etc., that float to the top. Drain and pat with a paper towel. Chop the shrimp. Trim the pork and slice it into slivers.

Heat the 6 Tbs. peanut oil in a wok or a large, heavy skillet. Add the sprouts, shrimp, pork, celery, mushrooms and scallions to the hot oil and cook at a simmer for about 10 minutes, stirring all the time. Add the soy sauce, sherry, salt, sugar and cornstarch broth, increase heat, and stir for 2-3 minutes longer.

Strain the filling mixture into a bowl and allow to cool and drain. Return cooking oil to the wok or skillet.

Put about 2 Tbs. of the filling mixture in each wrapper and fold the ends over the mixture tightly. Brush each roll with the stiff egg white to seal, like an envelope.

Add more oil to the wok or skillet, at least 1½ cups, and heat. Fry the egg rolls in the hot oil for about 6 minutes each, turning once to brown all over. Remove to paper toweling to drain. Serve hot.

The wrappers can also be fried until golden and crispy and served as chips with soy sauce and duck sauce.

Makes about 15 egg rolls

SHRIMP TOAST

1 lb. medium-size shrimp, shelled, cleaned and finely chopped
3 scallions, finely chopped
1 clove garlic, crushed
¼ tsp. ground ginger
1 Tbs. soy sauce
¼ tsp. ground black pepper
8 thin slices of white bread, trimmed
2 cups peanut oil

In a mixing bowl, blend all the ingredients except the bread and oil until smooth and pasty. Lightly toast the bread slices and spread the shrimp mixture on them.

Heat the oil in a large skillet and deep-fry the shrimp toast until crisp and golden. Remove to paper toweling to drain, cut into triangles, and serve hot.

Serves 8-10

SKEWERED MEAT WITH PEANUT SAUCE

2 lbs. lamb, cut into 1½" chunks
2 Tbs. curry powder
1/3 tsp. ground chili pepper
2 cloves garlic, finely chopped
2 tomatoes, cut in wedges
3 onions, cut in ½" slices
1 tsp. lemon juice
2 tsp. honey
Salt to taste

Peanut Sauce:
¾ cup coconut milk
¾ cup smooth peanut butter
1 Tbs. soy sauce
1 tsp. lemon juice
¾ Tbs. Worcestershire sauce
Dash of ground hot pepper
Salt to taste

Combine the lamb chunks with the remaining ingredients and allow to marinate for ½ hour, stirring several times.

Thread the meat on skewers alternately with tomato wedges and onion slices. Brown in the oven or on a barbecue grill for 15-20 minutes, turning once.

To make the peanut sauce, blend all the ingredients thoroughly until smooth. Pour over the hot skewered meat and serve.

Serves 4-6

PORK KEBABS WITH SAUCE

1 lb. pork loin,
cut into 1″ cubes
Juice of 1 lemon
1 clove garlic, crushed
1/3 tsp. chili powder
1¼ tsp. ground cumin
3 tsp. ground coriander
5 tsp. soy sauce
2 Tbs. peanut butter

Sauce:
¼ cup pineapple juice
¾ cup soy sauce
1 Tbs. Worcestershire sauce
1 Tbs. sherry
2 cloves garlic, finely chopped
1 tsp. ground ginger

Marinate the pork cubes for at least 1 hour in a paste made of the remaining ingredients. Make sure the cubes are covered on all sides.

Skewer the cubes and broil or barbecue for 25 minutes, until brown and tender.

To make the sauce, combine all the ingredients in a saucepan and bring to a boil. Remove from heat, strain and serve with the pork, accompanied by rice.

Serves 4

ZESTY MEATBALLS

½ lb. ground pork
½ lb. ground beef
¼ cup chopped onion
¼ cup chopped mushrooms
2 Tbs. soy sauce
¼ tsp. salt
⅛ tsp. black pepper
½ cup breadcrumbs
1 Tbs. grape jelly
1 egg, lightly beaten
1 clove garlic, chopped
2 Tbs. flour
1½ cups vegetable oil

Combine the meats, onions, mushrooms, seasonings, breadcrumbs, jelly, egg and garlic. When the mixture is well blended, form into balls about 1½" in diameter.

Spread flour on a board and roll the meatballs in it to coat all over. Heat oil very hot, add floured meatballs, and cook until browned and done through, about 8 minutes. Turn frequently while cooking.

Remove meatballs with a slotted spoon and drain. Serve with chutney and Chinese mustard.

Serves 10-12

BROILED SPARERIBS

2 lbs. spareribs
½ cup soy sauce
½ cup Major Grey's chutney, cut into small pieces
¼ cup honey
¼ tsp. salt
⅛ tsp. cayenne pepper
⅛ tsp. turmeric
2 cloves garlic, minced
2 Tbs. lemon juice

Thoroughly combine all the ingredients to make a marinade for the ribs. Marinate the ribs for at least an hour, turning often.

Broil or barbecue the ribs for 1-1¼ hours. Turn the ribs frequently during cooking and brush with marinade. Serve with chutney, rice and broiled tomatoes.

Serves 8

COCONUT SHRIMP ON BISCUITS

1 lb. shrimp, shelled, cleaned and cut into small pieces
½ cup chicken stock
Salt and pepper to taste
¼ cup milk
¼ cup slivered coconut meat
1 onion, chopped
1 clove garlic, minced
½ red pepper, chopped
½ green pepper, chopped
½ celery stalk, chopped
⅛ cup chopped seedless raisins
2 tsp. soy sauce
1 Tbs. olive oil

Boil the shrimp in the stock with salt and pepper for 3 minutes. Drain and set aside.

Put the milk and coconut meat in a saucepan and bring to a boil. Allow to cool for ½ hour.

Place the onion, garlic, peppers, celery, raisins, and soy sauce in a skillet and fry in the olive oil until onions are golden. Drain off the oil, then mix in the cooled coconut meat and milk. Chill in refrigerator for 1 hour.

Spoon the boiled shrimp onto cream crackers or toasted English muffins. Cover with the refrigerated sauce and serve.

Serves 6-8

2
Soups

Soups are important in the cuisine of the Orient. Bird's Nest, Wonton and Egg Drop are famous soups of Hong Kong and China, and the soups of Japan are different and delicious.

Soups are a regular part of most Japanese meals. The Japanese enjoy the bean paste soups even at breakfast, and the clear consommé-type soups are generally served either before or after dinner. Soups prepared with chicken, seafood and meats are also very popular.

Dashi, Japan's basic soup stock, is made from kelp (seaweed) and dried bonito. It is used in making almost all the Japanese soups.

You can create your own variations on the dashi soups by adding whatever garnishes you wish. Scallions, chopped and sprinkled on these clear soups, add flavor and look good. Carrots specially cut into pine tree shapes make an attractive garnish. You can also add spinach, sprouts and other vegetables, boiled shrimp, flaked fish, clams or mussels. All you need to make unique soups is a creative touch.

In the following pages you will find an interesting and flavorful group of Japanese and Oriental soups. They are easy to prepare and a joy to serve.

DASHI
A Soup Stock

5½ cups cold water
1 4″-square seaweed cake
½ cup flaked dried bonito

Put the water in a 2-qt. soup pot, bring to a boil, then lower to a simmer. Cut the seaweed cake into ½″ pieces, add to water, and cook at a moderate temperature for 2 minutes, uncovered. Remove seaweed with a slotted spoon and reserve.

Bring the liquid back to a boil, stir in the flaked bonito and cook for 1 minute. Remove from heat and let stand for a few minutes. Strain the broth into another pot through a mesh or cheesecloth. Reserve bonito.

The stock is now ready to be used in recipes calling for dashi. The reserved seaweed and bonito can be saved and used again.

Makes 1 qt.

JAPANESE EGG DROP SOUP

3 cups dashi
¼ tsp. salt
1 tsp. soy sauce
1 Tbs. cornstarch dissolved in
 2 Tbs. lukewarm water
1 egg, lightly beaten
 with 1 Tbs. cold dashi
Scant Tbs. ginger juice
Lime peel for garnish

Bring the dashi to a boil, covered. Stir in the salt, soy sauce and dissolved cornstarch. Lower heat and simmer until the soup begins to thicken and becomes smooth.

Using a fine sieve, pour the egg mixture in a circular motion over the top of the soup and cook until the egg begins to spin fine threads. Remove from heat.

Put a few drops of ginger juice in each soup bowl and ladle out the soup. Garnish each serving with a piece of lime peel cut in the shape of a pine tree.

Serves 4

VEGETABLE SOUP

½ lb. raw fresh spinach
1 small carrot
5 small taro roots
1 large white potato
1 8-oz. bean curd cake
2 Tbs. sesame oil
1 qt. dashi
¼ cup miso

Wash spinach and boil in salted water for 1 minute. Drain and pat dry with paper towels. Rinse several times in cold water, drain and press out water. Roll spinach into a thick roll and cut into 1″ pieces. Set aside.

Scrape the carrot and cut into 1″ pieces. Peel the taros and slice thin. Peel the potato, cut into thick slices and soak in cold water. Cook carrots, taros and potato slices in boiling water for 5 minutes. Drain and set aside.

Rinse the bean curd cake in warm water, dry with a cloth towel, wrap the cloth around it and crush the cake well. Heat sesame oil in a large pot and sauté bean curd for 2 minutes. Remove bean curd to a bowl, add 2 Tbs. of the dashi, and mash into a smooth paste with a pestle.

Add remaining dashi to the sesame oil in the pot, stir, add the vegetables and bring to a boil. Stir in the bean paste and miso, and blend thoroughly. Lower heat to a simmer and cook, covered, for 20 minutes.

Place the pieces of spinach roll in individual bowls, ladle in the soup and serve.

Serves 4-6

VEGETABLE AND FRIED BEAN CURD SOUP

6 dried mushrooms
1/8 tsp. sugar
1/2 burdock root
1 carrot, sliced
1 cup sliced white radish
5 small taro roots, quartered
1 bean curd cake
1 Tbs. peanut oil
1 qt. dashi
3/4 cup Japanese noodles
1 tsp. salt
1 Tbs. soy sauce
1 tsp. arrowroot
mixed with 1 Tbs. dashi
1 Tbs. chopped flat parsley
for garnish

Cover the mushrooms with water, add sugar and soak for 30 minutes. Squeeze dry and quarter. Scrape the burdock root, soak in cold water for 30 minutes and slice. Boil the mushrooms, burdock root, carrot, radish and taro roots in water to cover for 3 minutes. Drain and set aside.

Fry the bean curd cake in peanut oil for about 3 minutes. Rinse in hot water, drain and cut into 1/2"-thick slices.

Bring the dashi to a boil in a large pot with a cover, lower to a simmer, and add the vegetables and roots, bean curd, noodles, salt and soy sauce. Stir in the arrowroot mixture.

Cover the pot and simmer for about 15 minutes, or until vegetables are tender. Stir, garnish with chopped parsley and serve.

Serves 4-6

CHILLED CONSOMMÉ WITH ROLLED EGG, HAM, CHICKEN AND CUCUMBER

2 eggs
¼ tsp. salt
1 Tbs. unsalted butter
1 large cucumber
3 thin slices of cooked ham
1½ cups thinly sliced cooked chicken breast
1 qt. chicken consommé
1 tsp. soy sauce

Beat eggs with salt, melt butter in a crêpe pan or small round frying pan, and fry eggs to make 4–6 thin, flat pancakes. Keep the pancakes thin by twirling the pan and pouring back excess egg, as for an omelette. Fry until golden on both sides. Remove pancakes to a dinner plate, roll each pancake tightly and cut into 3 pieces.

Peel and slice cucumber, removing seedy center portion. Cut ham and chicken slices into strips.

Heat consommé to just under a boil and stir in soy sauce. Remove from heat, allow to cool, and place in refrigerator to chill. Arrange the egg rolls, cucumbers, ham and chicken in individual bowls, pour the chilled consommé over them and serve.

Serves 6–8

THICK PORK SOUP

1 lb. boneless pork loin, trimmed and coarsely ground
2 burdock roots
1 cup cubed sweet potato
1 carrot, scraped
1 medium-size potato, cubed
½ cup sliced white turnip
1″ piece of fresh ginger, sliced
1 Tbs. cornstarch smoothed into a paste with 1 Tbs. chicken broth
¼ cup white miso
1 Tbs. soy sauce
2 scallions, chopped, for garnish

Place pork in a colander or large wire strainer, pour boiling water over it, and allow to drain. Rinse with cold water and allow to drain.

In a large soup pot with a cover, bring a quart of water to a boil. Add pork and cook for about 3 minutes, skimming the fat off the top several times. Add all the vegetables, stir and simmer for 10 minutes, covered. Add the cornstarch paste, miso and soy sauce, and stir.

Cover the pot and cook soup at a slow simmer for about 2 hours, removing cover for the last 15 minutes. Serve garnished with chopped scallions and have Oriental 7 spices on hand for seasoning.

Serves 6

CLEAR CHICKEN BROTH WITH OKRA AND GINGER

2 okras
1 2″ piece of ginger root
1 12-oz. can of chicken broth
1 chicken bouillon cube
1 1″ square of kelp
¼ tsp. salt
¼ tsp. light soy sauce

Boil okras for 5 minutes, drain, trim, and cut each into 4 pieces. Cut ginger root into thin slices along grain, soak in cold water for 3 minutes and drain.

Put chicken broth in a saucepan with the bouillon cube, stir and bring to a boil. Lower heat, cover saucepan and cook at a low simmer for a few minutes.

Clean kelp with a damp cloth. Using cooking tongs, swish kelp in the soup about 6 times. Add salt and soy sauce, stir, cover the saucepan and cook for an additional 10 minutes.

Put okra pieces and ginger slices in individual bowls, ladle the hot soup over them, and serve.

Serves 4

CLEAR SOUP WITH OKRA AND BEAN CURD

4 small okras
2 cups dashi
½ tsp. salt
¼ tsp. light soy sauce
1 6-oz. bean curd cake

Boil okras in salted water for 5 minutes. Drain, trim the ends and chop finely. Place in a bowl and stir with a wooden spoon for 3 minutes to bring out the sticky okra juice. Reserve.

Put dashi in a saucepan with salt and soy sauce and bring to a low simmer. Cut bean curd cake into 4 equal parts and add to soup. Continue cooking at a simmer for 3 minutes.

Remove curds to individual bowls with a large slotted spoon. Spread a topping of okra over each curd, ladle in the hot soup and serve.

Serves 4

NOODLE SOUP LACED WITH SHERRY

1 oz. somen
6 large green beans
3 cups dashi
¼ tsp. salt
1 tsp. light soy sauce
¼ cup dry sherry

Boil noodles in salted water for a few minutes. Rinse with cold water, drain and reserve.

Boil green beans in salted water for 5 minutes. Rinse with cold water, trim ends, and cut each bean diagonally into 4 pieces.

In a saucepan stir together the dashi, salt, soy sauce and sherry. Bring to a boil, lower heat and simmer for 10 minutes.

Divide the noodles and beans equally into individual bowls, ladle the hot soup over them and serve.

Serves 4

MISO SOUP WITH SHELLFISH AND BEAN CURD

6 oz. miso
1 qt. dashi
1 dozen clams or mussels
1 2″-square bean curd cake, sliced into ½″ pieces
4 scallions, minced

Garnish:
½ oz. dried scallions with wakame
8 oz. dried scallions with tofu
1 oz. dried scallions with daikon

Fu and mustard
15 pressed wheatcake croutons
1 tsp. dry mustard mixed with enough water to make a thick paste

Place miso in a bowl and mash with a pestle until smooth. Bring dashi to a boil, remove from heat, and gradually add to the miso, stirring to mix well.

Strain mixture into a soup pot through a fine sieve and add shellfish, bean curd and scallions. Bring to a boil, stir, lower heat and cook until fish is tender, about 10 minutes. Serve at once with garnish sprinkled on.

Serves 4

CONSOMMÉ OVER FISH

4 dried black mushrooms
1 2-lb. fish fillet
Salt to taste
1 qt. dashi or clear broth
1 Tbs. soy sauce
4 strips of lemon peel

Soak the dried mushrooms in hot water for about 10 minutes. Drain and squeeze out the water.

Slice the fish fillet into 8 long strips, tie each strip into a bow-tie knot and salt. Steam for no longer than 5 minutes.

Bring dashi to a boil and season with soy sauce and more salt. Place 2 steamed fish ties, 1 mushroom and a strip of lemon peel in each serving bowl, ladle in the hot soup and serve.

Serves 4

SLICED BEEF AND YAM SOUP

2 cups raw grated yam
1 qt. dashi
1 lb. raw beef, thinly sliced
1 clove garlic, minced
2 scallions, chopped
1 Tbs. soy sauce
2 peppercorns
½ cup toasted chopped sesame seeds for garnish

Put the grated yam in a pot with the dashi. Stir and cook for 10 minutes over a low flame. Add the beef, garlic, scallions, soy sauce and peppercorns. Stir and cook for 10 more minutes.

Serve in heated bowls sprinkled with sesame seeds.

Serves 4

JAPANESE CHICKEN SOUP

1 Tbs. butter
½ cup chopped bamboo shoots
1 large onion, peeled and sliced
1 large potato, cut into small pieces
2 carrots, sliced
⅛ tsp. black pepper
1 5-lb. soup chicken, skinned, boned and thinly sliced
1 Tbs. soy sauce
1 Tbs. sherry
1 tsp. sugar
1 qt. dashi
1 chicken bouillon cube
1 tsp. cornstarch mixed with 1 tsp. hot dashi
½ tsp. grated ginger
2 scallion greens, minced, for garnish

Heat the butter in a skillet and sauté the bamboo shoots, onion, potato and carrots. Add the black pepper and stir. Cook for 4–5 minutes. Add the chicken and sauté for 3 minutes longer, turning frequently. Add the soy sauce, sherry and sugar and stir well.

Pour chicken mixture into a large soup pot and add dashi. Bring to a boil, lower the heat to a simmer, add bouillon cube and stir. Return to a boil and add the dissolved cornstarch, stirring slowly.

Cover the pot and cook for 15 minutes. Add grated ginger and stir well. Remove from stove and serve hot with a sprinkling of chopped scallions.

Serves 4-6

CHICKEN ORANGE-FLAVORED SOUP

4 orange peels, sliced
1½ Tbs. butter
1 Tbs. sugar
¼ cup grated white radish
½ cup orange juice
  or orange sauce
½ cup soy sauce
¼ cup sweet white wine
1 qt. chicken broth
1 chicken bouillon cube
1 3-4-lb. soup chicken
1 head Chinese cabbage,
  shredded
½ lb. fresh mushrooms, sliced
2 scallions, chopped, for garnish

Sauté the orange peels in the butter, turning often. Then add sugar and cook slowly until carmelized. Put the orange peels in a bowl with the radish, orange juice, soy sauce, and white wine. Mix and set aside to marinate.

In a large soup pot heat the chicken broth to a boil, stir in the bouillon cube and cook over low heat for about 3 minutes. Add the chicken, cover and cook slowly until chicken is tender. Add the cabbage and mushrooms, cover and cook for 15 minutes more.

Remove chicken to a heated platter and cut into serving portions. Pour the soup into heated bowls and sprinkle with scallions. Serve soup and chicken, with orange sauce on the side for the chicken.

Serves 4-6

SOUP WITH CHICKEN BALLS

1 4″ x 1″ seaweed cake
3 cups water
½ cup ground chicken
¾ Tbs. flour
1 bean curd cake, sliced
2 dried black mushrooms, soaked and sliced
½ Tbs. miso
3 fresh mushrooms, sliced
1 Tbs. light soy sauce
1 Tbs. finely chopped parsley
1 scallion, sliced
1 ½″ piece of ginger, grated

Clean the seaweed with a damp cloth and cut into ½″ cubes. Bring the water to a boil in a large pot, add seaweed and return to a boil. Remove kelp and discard, reserving broth.

Place the chicken in a mortar and pound with a pestle until light and fluffy. Add the flour and bean curd and pound until smooth. Blend in the dried sliced mushrooms.

Form the chicken mixture into small balls and drop into the reserved seaweed broth. Add the miso and stir. Add the fresh mushrooms, soy sauce, parsley and scallion and cook for a few minutes.

Cook until the chicken balls are done, stirring frequently. Place chicken balls in heated bowls and pour the soup over them. Squeeze the ginger and add some of the pulp and ginger juice to each bowl before serving.

Serves 4

MACKEREL SOUP
An Osaka Favorite

1 medium-size mackerel fillet
Salt to taste
1 3-oz. white radish, peeled
  and cut into julienne strips
1 4″ x 2″ seaweed cake, cubed
3 cups water
1 Tbs. soy sauce
Lime peel for garnish

Cut the fish diagonally into 4 portions. Salt and set aside for 30 minutes. Then cook in water to cover for 1 minute. Remove, rinse, in cold water, drain and set aside.

Cook the radish slowly in water to cover for 4 minutes. Drain. Clean seaweed with a damp cloth.

Put the radish, seaweed, fish, water and soy sauce in a soup pot, adding more salt if needed. Bring to a boil, reduce heat and cook slowly for 15 minutes. Serve the fish pieces and soup in heated bowls, garnished with lime peel. For a special Japanese decorative touch, cut the lime peels into pine tree shapes.

Serves 3-4

CABBAGE SOUP

2 cups shredded cabbage
2 tomatoes, minced
2 onions, minced
¼ tsp. salt
⅛ tsp. black pepper
¼ tsp. chopped chili pepper
1 tsp. blackberry jam
1 anchovy, mashed
1½ Tbs. vegetable oil
2 cloves garlic, chopped
¾ tsp. lemon juice
4 cups beef bouillon

In a large saucepan combine cabbage, tomatoes, onions, seasonings, jam, anchovy and oil. Stir in garlic and lemon juice. Simmer for 15 minutes.

Add bouillon, stir and cook slowly for 45 minutes, covered. Remove from heat, stir and serve.

Serves 4-6

CHILLED CREAM SOUP

2 celery stalks, chopped
3 onions, minced
1 apple, peeled, cored and chopped
¼ cup unsalted butter
2 Tbs. curry powder
3 Tbs. flour
4 cups chicken broth
1 chicken bouillon cube
⅛ tsp. ground chili pepper
¼ tsp. salt
2 cups cream
1 cup cooked shredded chicken
Shredded coconut for garnish

In a 2-qt. pot sauté the celery, onions and apple in the butter until onions are golden. Add curry powder and stir. Slowly mix in flour as you add chicken broth. Add bouillon cube and stir to dissolve.

Simmer until mixture thickens and is well blended, stirring all the time. Add chili pepper and salt and stir for 2 minutes longer. Remove from heat to cool.

Pour the cooled soup into an electric mixer or blender and blend until smooth. Place in refrigerator to chill. Before serving, stir in the cream and shredded chicken. Garnish with shredded coconut.

Serves 6

CHICKEN SOUP

½ cup salted butter
2 large onions, sliced
1 clove garlic, mashed
1 large hen, cut in half
¼ tsp. salt
⅛ tsp. white pepper
Dash each of chili pepper, cumin, turmeric and coriander, mixed
1 qt. chicken consommé
2 carrots, scraped and sliced
½ tsp. flour mixed into a paste with juice of ½ lemon

Melt butter in a large saucepan and sauté onions and garlic until onions are transparent. Add hen halves, salt and pepper, placing onion rings on top of the hen. Cover saucepan and cook at moderate heat for 20 minutes. Remove from heat and allow to cool.

Remove meat from bones and discard bones. Cut meat into small pieces and return to saucepan. Sprinkle mixed spices over meat, add consommé and carrots, stir and cook at a slow simmer for about 30 minutes or until meat is tender.

Add flour paste to soup and stir to thicken. Strain off the soup and serve with chicken meat and carrots.

Serves 4-6

PORK AND SCALLION SOUP

1 lb. lean pork, chopped
4 scallions, chopped
¼ tsp. salt
⅛ tsp. black pepper
¾ tsp. soy sauce
2 eggs, beaten
1 qt. chicken broth
Chopped flat parsley for garnish

Thoroughly mix the pork with the scallions, salt, pepper, soy sauce and eggs. Form into small meatballs.

Bring the chicken broth to a boil in a saucepan. Add meatballs, reduce heat, cover and cook for 1¼ hours. Serve in small bowls, garnished with parsley.

Serves 6

CELESTIAL SOUP

4 cups water
1 chicken bouillon cube
2 scallion whites, cut in rounds
1½ Tbs. soy sauce
½ tsp. salt
¾ tsp. vegetable oil
2 drops of sesame oil

Bring the water to a boil with the bouillon cube. Mix together the remaining ingredients and pour the boiling water and bouillon over them.

The "Soup for the Gods" is ready to serve. It is excellent for clearing the palate.

Serves 6

BIRD'S NEST SOUP

3 oz. bird's nest, soaked in water for 6–8 hours
Vegetable oil
3 cups chicken broth
2 slices of ginger
1 Tbs. sherry
⅛ tsp. pepper
1 chicken breast, boned and chopped
½ cup sliced Virginia ham
1 Tbs. cornstarch mixed with 1 Tbs. water
1 egg white, beaten
A few drops of sesame oil
Chopped parsley for garnish

Sprinkle the bird's nest with a little vegetable oil and wash in warm water. Repeat until clean, making sure to remove all the feathers.

Place the bird's nest and 2 cups of the chicken broth in a bowl. Add the ginger, sherry and pepper. Put the bowl in a steamer or double boiler and steam for 1 hour.

Pour the bird's nest broth into a saucepan and discard bird's nest. Add the chicken breast, ham and remaining chicken broth. Boil for 3 minutes. Lower heat, add the cornstarch mixture gradually and stir. Return to a boil.

Remove from heat, beat in the egg white, and sprinkle with ¼ tsp. vegetable oil and the sesame oil. Garnish with parsley.

Serves 4

GINGER BEEF SOUP

½ lb. chuck beef,
 cut into 1″ cubes
2 scallion whites, minced
3 cups water
1 Tbs. sherry
4 slices of fresh ginger
 or ½ tsp. ground ginger
Salt and pepper to taste
¼ lb. bean sprouts
Chopped parsley for garnish

Brown the meat with the scallions in a heavy saucepan. Add the water, sherry, ginger, salt and pepper, and simmer for 1½ hours. Add bean sprouts for the last ½ hour.

Serve hot, sprinkled with parsley.

Serves 4

MUSHROOM SOUP

2 egg whites
Salt and pepper to taste
1 Tbs. sherry
1 cup chicken broth
½ cup diced ham
1/3 cup green peas
¼ cup diced bamboo shoots
¼ lb. mushrooms, sliced
1 Tbs. cornstarch mixed
 with 1 Tbs. water
¼ tsp. salt
⅛ tsp. pepper

Beat the egg whites and add the salt and pepper to taste, sherry and ½ cup of the chicken broth. Mix and place in the top of a double boiler. Cook slowly for 20 minutes.

Add remaining chicken broth and bring to a boil. Add ham and cook for 3 minutes. Add green peas and bamboo shoots and cook for 3 minutes more. Add mushrooms and cook for 2 minutes. Stir in the cornstarch mixture to thicken. Add salt and pepper, stir and cook for 3 more minutes. Serve hot.

Serves 4

CHINESE EGG DROP SOUP

1 egg, beaten
¼ cup water
3 cups chicken consommé
¼ tsp. salt
½ tsp. sugar
1½ Tbs. cornstarch mixed smooth with ½ tsp. water
1 scallion, sliced, for garnish

Mix together egg and water. Bring consommé to a boil, add salt and sugar, and stir. Add cornstarch mixture and stir in to thicken the soup. Simmer for a few minutes, uncovered.

Remove from heat and gradually add the egg mixture, stirring constantly. Sprinkle with scallions and serve hot.

Serves 4

WONTON SOUP

4 dried black mushrooms
4 cups chicken broth
1 chicken breast
¼ lb. sliced ham
½ cup bamboo shoots
¼ lb. snow peas
1 scallion, chopped
16 wontons

Soak mushrooms in water to cover for 15 minutes. Drain, reserve mushrooms and add mushroom water to chicken broth. Cook chicken breast in broth at a simmer for 15 minutes.

Bone chicken and cut into thin strips. Cut ham, bamboo shoots, snow peas and mushrooms into small pieces.

Add chicken, ham, bamboo shoots and mushrooms to the broth and cook for 15 minutes over medium heat. Add snow peas, scallions and wontons, bring to a boil, and cook for 10 minutes more.

Serves 4

WINTER MELON SOUP

6 dried black mushrooms
1 medium winter melon
1 large chicken breast, boned and diced
½ lb. shrimp, shelled, cleaned and diced
¾ Tbs. cornstarch mixed with ⅛ cup water
3½ cups chicken stock
1/3 cup cubed bamboo shoots
3 slices fresh ginger
¼ cup sliced Virginia ham
Salt and pepper to taste

Soak the mushrooms in warm water for 20 minutes, drain, slice and reserve. Cut a slice off the melon 1¼″ from the top to use as a lid. Remove seeds and clean inside of melon.

Blend the diced chicken and shrimp with the cornstarch mixture and reserve. Bring the chicken stock to a boil.

Place melon in a heat-proof bowl, and place the bowl in a steamer in 1½ cups water. Pour the boiled chicken stock into the melon, then add the mushrooms, bamboo shoots, ginger and ham. Cover the steamer and steam for at least 1 hour, or until the melon is soft.

Add the chicken-shrimp-cornstarch mixture, salt and pepper to the soup in the melon, mix well, cover and steam for another 15 minutes. Remove the bowl with the melon and serve hot.

Serves 4-6

CHICKEN CORN SOUP

2 cups canned chicken broth
1 8-oz. can of creamed corn
½ cup water
¾ tsp. sherry
Salt and pepper to taste
1 large chicken breast, cooked, boned and minced
2 tsp. cornstarch mixed with ¼ cup water
1 egg, beaten

Put the chicken broth in a saucepan with the corn, water, sherry, salt and pepper. Bring to a boil and simmer for 5 minutes.

Add the chicken and the cornstarch mixture, stir until soup begins to thicken, then simmer for 10 more minutes, stirring often. Remove from heat and slowly blend in the beaten egg. Serve hot.

Serves 3-4

HOT AND SOUR SOUP

2 dried black mushrooms
1 cup water
½ cup shredded cooked pork
1/3 cup shredded bamboo shoots
3 water chestnuts, shredded
1 2″-square bean curd cake, sliced
1 Tbs. vinegar
¼ tsp. red pepper sauce or ground red pepper
1 Tbs. soy sauce
1 tsp. cornstarch mixed with 1¼ Tbs. water
1 egg, beaten

Soak mushrooms in warm water to cover for 15 minutes. Drain, save mushroom water, and slice mushrooms.

Add mushroom water to the 1 cup water and bring to a boil. Add mushrooms, pork, bamboo shoots and water chestnuts, and cook for 3 minutes.

Add bean curd, vinegar, pepper and soy sauce, return to a boil and slowly add cornstarch mixture, stirring until thick. Remove from heat and slowly mix in the egg.

Serves 2

CHICKEN SOUP WITH NOODLES

5 dried black mushrooms
2 cooked chicken breasts, boned and diced
1½ Tbs. soy sauce
½ tsp. sugar
Salt and pepper to taste
2 Tbs. peanut oil
2/3 cup bamboo shoots
4 cups chicken broth
½ lb. noodles
2 scallion whites, sliced, for garnish

Soak mushrooms for 10 minutes, drain, slice and reserve. Mix chicken with soy sauce, sugar, salt and pepper.

Heat oil in a large skillet, add chicken mixture, and stir-fry for 2 minutes. Add mushrooms and bamboo shoots and stir-fry for 2 minutes more.

Boil chicken broth, add stir-fried ingredients, return to a boil and simmer for 20 minutes. Meanwhile, boil noodles for 5 minutes and drain.

Ladle the soup into individual bowls, add noodles to each bowl, garnish with scallions and serve hot.

Serves 4

SHARK FIN SOUP

3 oz. shark fins
2 slices of fresh ginger
6 dried black mushrooms
1 large chicken breast, cooked, boned and sliced
¾ tsp. cornstarch mixed with 1 tsp. soy sauce
1 qt. chicken broth
½ cup sliced ham
Salt and pepper to taste
½ cup bamboo shoots
1½ Tbs. flour mixed with ⅛ cup water
1 egg, beaten

Soak shark fins in water for 6–8 hours, clean and rinse. Boil fins in water with the ginger, cover the pot, and cook at a simmer for ½ hour. Allow to cool with cover on, then drain, rinse and set aside.

Soak mushrooms in cold water for 15 minutes, drain, slice thin and reserve. Toss chicken slices with cornstarch mixture and reserve.

Bring chicken broth to a boil in a soup pot. Add shark fins, ham, salt and pepper. Simmer for 1 hour, covered.

Add mushrooms and bamboo shoots and simmer for 5 minutes more. Add chicken mixture, stir lightly and simmer for 2 minutes. Add flour mixed with water and continue to stir until thick. Gradually add the egg, stirring until smooth.

Remove from stove and serve hot.

Serves 4–6

CRAB MEAT AND CORN SOUP

1 qt. canned chicken broth
1 12-oz. can of creamed corn
¼ tsp. ground ginger
⅛ tsp. cayenne pepper
½ tsp. light soy sauce
1 cup diced crab meat
1 Tbs. dry sherry
1 celery stalk, thinly sliced
1½ tsp. cornstarch
1 egg white

Put broth in a soup pot and bring to a boil. Stir in the corn and ginger, lower heat and simmer for 8 minutes.

Stir in the cayenne, soy sauce, crab meat, sherry and celery. Simmer for 5 minutes, then slowly add the cornstarch, stirring to dissolve and blend.

Turn off heat and let stand, covered, for 5 minutes. Slowly stir in the egg white and serve.

Serves 4

CHICKEN GINGER SOUP

1 qt. water
1 3-4-lb. chicken
3 celery stalks,
  cut into 4″ pieces
2 large carrots, cut lengthwise
Salt and pepper to taste
1 1″ piece of fresh ginger
1 Tbs. peanut oil
2 large onions, minced
¾ cup bean sprouts
4 hard-boiled eggs, sliced
Lemon slices for garnish

In a large soup pot bring water to a boil. Add chicken, celery, carrots, salt and pepper. Cover the pot and cook for 1 hour or until chicken is tender.

With a slotted spoon remove celery and carrots and reserve. Add ginger. Remove chicken to cool. Skin, bone and slice.

Heat the oil and sauté the onions until golden brown. Add bean sprouts and sauté for about 6 minutes longer.

Place chicken slices in individual soup bowls along with the reserved celery and carrots and the sautéed onions and bean sprouts. Top with slices of egg and ladle the soup over each serving. Garnish with lemon slices.

Serves 4

CLAM SOUP

1 Tbs. sesame oil
½ cup ground pork
1 tsp. cornstarch
1 Tbs. soy sauce
¼ tsp. salt
⅛ tsp. black pepper
½ tsp. ground ginger
1 celery stalk, thinly sliced
2 cups clam juice
6 clams
½ cup thinly sliced boiled ham

Heat oil in a saucepan. Add pork, cornstarch, soy sauce, salt, pepper and ginger. Sauté and stir until pork is slightly browned. Add celery and sauté for 1 minute more.

Add clam juice and simmer for about 15 minutes, stirring frequently. Meanwhile, cook clams in water to cover for a few minutes and then mince. Add clams and ham to saucepan and simmer for 5 minutes more. Stir and serve hot.

Serves 4

HOT AND SOUR SOUP

1 qt. chicken consommé
2 tsp. lemon juice
½ tsp. crushed chili pepper
2 tsp. soy sauce
1 medium-size onion, chopped
1 clove garlic, minced
⅛ tsp. coriander
2 cooked chicken breasts, skinned, boned and shredded
1 cup cooked thin noodles

In a soup pot mix all the ingredients except the chicken and noodles. Bring to a boil and add chicken. Lower heat and simmer slowly for 15 minutes.

Put equal portions of the noodles in individual bowls, ladle in the soup and serve hot.

Serves 4-6

COCONUT SOUP

1 large coconut
4 cups chicken consommé
½ tsp. mace
½ tsp. coriander
2 egg yolks, well beaten
1 Tbs. flour

Grate the coconut meat and reserve the milk. Boil the meat in water for 3 minutes, strain and set aside.

Heat the consommé and add the coconut milk, mace and coriander. Squeeze the juice from the coconut meat, add juice to soup along with 2 Tbs. of the squeezed meat, and stir. Discard remaining coconut meat. Simmer soup for 35 minutes, covered.

Meanwhile, make a smooth paste of the egg yolks, flour and 2 Tbs. of the soup. When soup is done, mix in the paste and cook for 2 minutes longer. Serve with plain crackers.

Serves 4

CREAMED SHRIMP SOUP

3 cups milk
3 cups heavy cream
2½ cups grated coconut
3 cloves garlic, minced
1 small onion, chopped
2 Tbs. honey
1 Tbs. anchovy paste
2 tsp. soy sauce
2 Tbs. grated lemon rind
1/3 tsp. ground chili pepper
½ tsp. ground coriander
Salt and pepper to taste
1 lb. medium-size shrimp, shelled and cleaned
1½ Tbs. chopped parsley for garnish

In a large soup pot combine the milk, cream and coconut and bring to a boil. Remove from heat and strain through a fine sieve, returning liquid to pot. Press juice from coconut meat, discard pressed meat, add juice to pot and simmer for 5 minutes, stirring.

In a large bowl combine all the remaining ingredients except the shrimp and parsley. Pound the mixture until well blended and reduced to a smooth paste.

Add the coconut cream mixture and shrimp to the bowl, mix with the paste, and return entire mixture to the soup pot. Cook at a low simmer for 10 minutes and serve with a sprinkling of parsley.

Serves 6-8

3
Eggs

The French have their omelettes, the Italians their frittas, and indeed, most of the countries of the world have their egg specialties—a whole range of dishes, from plain to stuffed to flaming delights. Japan is no exception.

The Japanese have developed egg cookery into an art form. They use eggs fried thin and sliced in many dishes, even to top noodles, they make omelettes rolled with tasty meats or vegetables, and their egg custards are imaginative and delicious.

Japan's egg dishes are distinctive and different, but *different* does not mean *difficult*. The recipes in this chapter—as well as many fine egg recipes included in other chapters—are delicious and easy to make. So let's take to the skillet and chopsticks and prepare some delightful egg cookery. Tempt your guests with egg magic—they'll love it.

CHAWAN-MUSHI
An Egg Custard with Chicken and Shrimp

4 dried black mushrooms
¼ cup thinly sliced cooked chicken
4 shrimp, quickly boiled, shelled, cleaned and roughly chopped
½ tsp. sake
1¼ tsp. soy sauce
4 cooked spinach leaves, shredded
8 canned ginkgo nuts, chopped
4 slices of kamaboko
3 eggs
3 cups dashi
¼ tsp. salt

Soak mushrooms in sugared water for 2 hours. Drain, squeeze out moisture, trim off stems and slice caps.

Preheat oven to 450°.

In a mixing bowl combine mushrooms, chicken and shrimp with sake and soy sauce. Mix well and blend in shredded spinach. Mix in ginkgo nuts and kamaboko slices.

Beat the eggs lightly with dashi and salt. Add to the chicken-shrimp mixture and blend well.

Spoon the mixture into 4 8-oz. heat-resistant custard cups. Make sure each cup is no more than ¾ full. Cover each cup with aluminum foil and slit to allow steam to escape.

Place cups in a pan of steaming hot water. Cups should be ¾ immersed in water. Lower oven heat to 375°-400° and place pan in oven. Bake for 20 minutes, or until custard sets. Remove custard cups and serve cooled or chilled.

Serves 4

SHRIMP IN EGGS

12 shrimp, shelled, cleaned and finely chopped
½ cup chicken broth
½ tsp. salt
1 tsp. arrowroot
3 eggs, lightly beaten with chopsticks
½ tsp. sugar
½ Tbs. dry sherry
1 Tbs. sunflower oil or vegetable oil

Press the chopped shrimp with the flat of a knife to make a smooth paste. Boil chicken broth with salt and stir in the shrimp paste. Cook for 1 minute, allow to cool, strain through a fine mesh, and remove shrimp to a plate.

Mix arrowroot with 1 tsp. of the broth, saving the rest of the broth to use as stock. Beat eggs with arrowroot, sugar and sherry. Add shrimp and mix well.

Heat oil in a large omelette pan. Pour in the egg mixture, rotating pan so that the entire bottom is covered. Fry over moderate heat until golden brown on one side, then turn and fry on the other side until golden brown.

Remove omelette to a plate, roll, and slice into ½" pieces. Serve as an appetizer or as a main course with spinach.

Serves 6

SPINACH-STUFFED EGG ROLLS

1¼ cups chopped cooked spinach
½ Tbs. soy sauce
2 eggs
1 tsp. sugar
¼ tsp. sake
¼ tsp. salt
Peanut oil for frying

Heat spinach slightly and mix with a little of the soy sauce. Tightly press the spinach to make two rolls. Set spinach rolls aside.

Lightly beat the eggs with the remaining soy sauce and the sugar, sake and salt.

Heat peanut oil in an omelette pan, add half the egg mixture and fry until bottom is golden brown and top sets. Do not turn. Slide the omelette over one of the spinach rolls, then roll omelette and spinach together. Make another omelette with the remaining egg mixture and roll it around the other spinach roll.

Cut each roll in half and serve.

Serves 4

STUFFED EGGS WITH RED SALMON ROE

6 hard-boiled eggs
1 tsp. soy sauce
3 mushroom caps, finely chopped
1 scallion white, finely chopped
4 oz. red salmon roe

Cut the eggs in half lengthwise, remove yolks to a bowl, and reserve whites.

Mash egg yolks and soy sauce into a smooth paste. Blend in mushrooms, scallions and 1 oz. of the salmon roe.

Stuff the egg whites with the yolk mixture and garnish with the remaining caviar.

This dish makes the perfect accompaniment to Kirin beer.

Serves 6

EGGS WITH CHICKEN LIVERS

2 Tbs. soy sauce
1 Tbs. dry sherry
1 tsp. sugar
½ tsp. salt
⅛ tsp. cayenne pepper
1 lb. chicken livers
1 Tbs. sesame oil
3 eggs
1 tsp. soy sauce
1 tsp. duck sauce

Blend the 2 Tbs. soy sauce with the sherry, sugar, salt and cayenne to make a marinade. Marinate the livers for ½ hour.

Heat the oil in a frying pan until very hot. Add the marinated livers and sauté for 8 minutes, turning and stirring. Remove livers to paper toweling to drain. Reserve oil.

Lightly beat the eggs with the 1 tsp. soy sauce and duck sauce. Reheat the oil, adding more if needed. Return livers to pan and pour in egg mixture. Cook at moderate heat until bottom is browned and top sets.

Fold the egg pancake over and cut into 4 portions. Serve with cooked asparagus and cooked tomatoes.

Serves 4

EGGS WITH PORK AND SPINACH

1 Tbs. peanut oil
½ lb. loin of pork, sliced
1 onion, sliced
1 clove garlic, minced
½ green pepper, minced
½ red pepper, minced
1 Tbs. chopped ginger
3 eggs
½ Tbs. soy sauce
1 tsp. sweet sherry
¼ tsp. salt
1 tsp. pineapple preserves
½ cup cooked spinach

Heat the oil in a frying pan and add the pork, onion, garlic, peppers and ginger. Cook for about 20 minutes, stirring and turning often.

Lightly beat the eggs with the soy sauce, sherry, salt and preserves. When pork is tender, remove pork mixture from pan. Pour egg mixture into pan, return pork mixture over eggs and add spinach.

Cook at moderate heat until top sets. Cut into 4 portions and serve hot.

Serves 4

STUFFED EGG ROLLS WITH VEGETABLES

1 lb. chicken livers, cut in half
¼ lb. raw chicken, sliced
2 Tbs. flour
2 Tbs. peanut oil
3 cloves garlic, finely chopped
3 scallions (whites and 3″ of greens), chopped
½ tsp. ground ginger
4 eggs
½ tsp. soy sauce
¼ tsp. salt
1 Tbs. sweet sherry

Vegetables:
½ lb. stringbeans, trimmed, cut diagonally into 3 pieces and cooked
3 carrots, sliced and cooked
1 white turnip, cubed and cooked
3 medium-size potatoes, cubed and cooked

Sauce:
2 Tbs. soy sauce
2 Tbs. duck sauce
2 Tbs. sherry

Dredge the livers and chicken in the flour. Heat the oil in a frying pan until hot and sauté the livers and chicken until chicken is tender. Turn to brown all over. Remove to a dish.

Sauté the garlic, scallions and ginger in the remaining oil until scallions turn golden. Remove ingredients with a slotted spoon and drain.

Lightly beat the eggs with the soy sauce, salt and sherry. Fry the egg mixture in the frying pan to make 3 round pancakes, 8″ in diameter, browned on both sides.

Spoon the garlic, scallions and ginger over the pancakes, then the livers and chicken. Roll the pancakes and cut each into 6–8 equal parts. Serve on plates with the cooked vegetables.

To make the sauce, mix all the ingredients and pour into sauce servers to accompany the meal.

Serves 6–8

4
Noodles and Rice

Japanese noodles come in a wide variety of styles and shapes. The three best-known kinds are *soba,* slender green noodles made from buckwheat flour; *somen,* thin wheat vermicelli, and *udon,* thick noodles made from either wheat flour or corn flour.

The Japanese are very fond of noodles. They eat them hot or cold, topped with various sauces, foods and condiments. No matter what food is served with them, Japanese noodles retain their distinctive flavor, especially in soups and side dishes.

A basic recipe for cooking wheat noodles or flat wide noodles appears on p. 71. For other types of noodles, consult your grocer or the package instructions. Cooked noodles can always be served with any of the chicken or dashi broths from the soup chapter poured over them.

The rice of Japan is a short-grain rice very close to the Chinese variety. It is also similar to Eastern European pilaf, the main difference lying in the sake that is added to most Japanese rice recipes. The consistency of cooked Japanese rice is thick but pleasant, never pasty.

Rice is a staple of the Japanese cuisine. It is served at almost every meal, in between meals, and as an accompaniment to most other dishes. Mixed with vegetables, fish or meat, it is a meal in itself.

Basic recipes for cooked rice and Japanese boiled rice appear on p. 73. In recipes that call for Japanese rice, you can substitute any other short-grain rice.

Japanese rice and noodles are available in the United States in many large supermarkets and in Oriental groceries or specialty shops.

BASIC COOKED NOODLES

2 cups wheat noodles or flat wide noodles
4 cups water
Salt to taste

Cook the noodles in 1 cup of salted water. When the water boils, add another cup of water and return to a boil. Repeat with the remaining 2 cups of water.

Boil the noodles until tender, not pasty. Do not overcook. Drain the noodles, run under hot water, and drain again.

Makes 2 cups cooked noodles

COLD WHEAT VERMICELLI

1 lb. thin vermicelli
2 cups chicken broth
½ cup soy sauce
3 Tbs. sake
1 Tbs. sugar
¼ tsp. grated ginger

In a saucepan cover the vermicelli with the chicken broth. Bring to a boil, then lower heat to a constant simmer. Stir and cook until tender. Drain the vermicelli and save the broth. Rinse vermicelli under cold water, drain, put into a chilled bowl and refrigerate.

Combine the reserved chicken broth with the soy sauce, sake, sugar and ginger. Bring to a boil. Lower heat and cook at a simmer for 3 minutes. Stir. Allow to cool, then chill in refrigerator.

Serve the noodles in individual bowls and put chilled sauce in small dishes for dipping. If you like, garnish noodles with cherry tomatoes, cucumber sticks and thinly sliced green peppers.

Serves 6

JAPANESE GARDEN FAN

½ lb. buckwheat noodles
2½ cups salted water
¼ cup chicken broth
2 Tbs. soy sauce
1¼ tsp. sugar
5 dried black mushrooms, soaked for 2-3 hours, drained, trimmed and sliced
¼ tsp. salt
4 eggs
¼ lb. cooked ham, thinly sliced and cut into 3″ strips
1 cucumber, peeled and sliced lengthwise into strips
1 cup chopped cooked spinach
2 red peppers, sliced into strips and sautéed
4 scallions (whites and 1″ length of greens), sliced into strips
12 whole cherry or plum tomatoes

Sauce:
¼ cup white wine vinegar
1 tsp. dry sherry
1 tsp. sesame oil
½ cup soy sauce
¼ cup dashi or clear chicken broth
2 Tbs. sugar

Prepare the sauce first. Combine all ingredients, beat to blend, and bring to a boil in a saucepan. Lower heat to a simmer and cook for 5 minutes, stirring. Set sauce aside.

Cook the buckwheat noodles in the salted water until slightly soft. Drain, rinse in hot water, and drain again. Place noodles in the center of individual serving plates.

In a saucepan stir together the chicken broth, soy sauce and 1 tsp. of the sugar. Bring to a boil, then lower heat and add mushrooms. Simmer for 2½ minutes. Drain mushrooms and reserve.

Lightly beat the remaining ¼ tsp. sugar and the salt with the eggs. Oil a large frying pan and fry the egg mixture to make several thin pancakes, lightly browned on both sides. Cut egg pancakes into strips.

Fan the egg, ham and vegetables around the noodles to make a colorful display. Ladle the sauce over the noodles and serve.

Serves 6-8

BASIC COOKED RICE

2 cups rice
2½ cups water

Wash the rice thoroughly. Put it in a covered pot with the water and boil slowly until tender.

Makes 3–4 cups cooked rice

JAPANESE BOILED RICE

1 cup rice
1½ cups water

Wash the rice and drain, repeating the procedure until the drained water is clear.

Place the rice and water in a heavy pot with a tight-fitting cover. Bring to a boil until steam begins to rise from the sides of the cover, about 5 minutes.

Once steam begins to escape, lower the heat and simmer for 10 minutes. Then lower the heat again and simmer for 10 minutes more. Turn the heat off and, without touching the cover, allow the rice to stand for 10 minutes. Serve at once.

Makes 2 cups boiled rice

RICE TOPPED WITH BATTERED SHRIMP

8 large shrimp or prawns
1½ cup Japanese rice
2 cups dashi or chicken broth
½ tsp. salt
1 cup peanut oil for frying
Chopped chives for garnish

Batter:
2 eggs, lightly beaten
1 cup flour
½ cup milk
Salt and pepper to taste

Sauce:
1 cup dashi
½ cup soy sauce
1 Tbs. sake
½ Tbs. dry sherry
2 tsp. sugar

Place shrimp in water and bring to a boil. Remove shrimp and peel down to the tails. Split and clean, leaving tails intact.

Cook the rice with the dashi and salt until tender. Place a bed of rice in each of 4 serving bowls.

Prepare the batter by combining all the ingredients. Dip shrimp in batter and deep-fry in the peanut oil until golden. Place 2 shrimp in each bowl on top of the rice.

To make the sauce, combine all the ingredients in a saucepan, bring to a slow simmer and stir for about 2 minutes to blend well.

Pour a little of the hot sauce over the shrimp and rice in each bowl and garnish with chives. Put the rest of the sauce in small sauce dishes for each guest.

Serves 4

RICE COOKED IN GREEN TEA

1¼ Tbs. green tea
2 cups water
1 cup Japanese rice
1 Tbs. sake
1 Tbs. dry sherry
¼ tsp. salt
2 dashes of lemon juice

Tie the tea securely in a piece of cheesecloth to make a small teabag. Bring the water to a boil in a saucepan, add teabag and lower heat to a strong simmer. Cook for 3 minutes. Remove and discard teabag.

Stir in the rice, then stir in the remaining ingredients. Cover with a tight-fitting lid and cook until the liquid steams. Lower heat and cook for 10 minutes. Stir, lower heat again, replace lid and steam for 10 minutes more. Remove saucepan from heat and allow to stand for 10 minutes, covered. Serve rice in bowls, hot.

Serves 4

BOILED RICE WITH SHELLFISH

1 cup chicken broth
1 chicken bouillon cube
12 oysters or clams, shucked and washed
1½ cups Japanese boiled rice (see p. 73)

Sauce:
1 Tbs. soy sauce
1 tsp. lemon juice
1 tsp. sake
2 Tbs. plum wine

Bring chicken broth to a boil. Add bouillon cube and stir to dissolve. Add oysters and lower heat to a slow simmer. Cook for no more than 5 minutes.

Place rice in small bowls and top with cooked oysters.

Prepare the sauce by mixing all the ingredients thoroughly. Serve in small dipping dishes to accompany rice.

Serves 4

BOILED RICE WITH MUSHROOMS

1½ cups Japanese boiled rice (see p. 73)
1 lb. fresh mushrooms, sliced

Sauce:
1 Tbs. soy sauce
2 Tbs. blackberry brandy
1 tsp. lemon juice

Prepare rice according to instructions. During the last 10 minutes of cooking, stir in mushrooms.

To make the sauce, mix all the ingredients well. Place rice and mushrooms in individual bowls, spoon on some of the sauce, and serve the rest of the sauce on the side.

Serves 4-6

RICE WITH BAMBOO SHOOTS

2 cups Japanese boiled rice (see p. 73)
1 cup chopped cooked bamboo shoots
2 Tbs. soy sauce
1 Tbs. sake

Combine rice with bamboo shoots and blend well. Stir together soy sauce and sake, pour over rice and shoots, and serve hot.

Serves 4

RICE WITH VEGETABLES AND SEAWEED

½ lb. stringbeans
½ lb. asparagus tips
6 seaweed leaves
2 cups cooked rice
(see p. 73; substitute dashi or chicken broth for water)

Sauce:
2 Tbs. soy sauce
2 Tbs. plum wine
1 Tbs. sake

Boil stringbeans and asparagus tips in salted water until tender but still crisp. Drain, trim stringbeans, and cut each bean diagonally into 3-4 pieces. Thoroughly mix beans, asparagus and seaweed leaves with rice.

Mix sauce ingredients and pour sauce over rice mixture. Heat and serve.

Serves 6

RICE WITH GREEN VEGETABLES AND ALMONDS

2 cups Japanese boiled rice or long-grain boiled rice
(see p. 73; substitute dashi or chicken broth for water)
½ cup boiled spinach
½ cup sliced cooked green beans
¼ cup cooked petits pois
1 cup shredded lettuce
½ cup cooked diced celery
¼ tsp. salt
½ tsp. chopped green pepper
1 Tbs. grated radish
2 Tbs. soy sauce
1 Tbs. sake
1 tsp. sugar
½ Tbs. slivered almonds
for garnish

Thoroughly mix rice with vegetables, salt, green pepper and radish. Combine soy sauce, sake and sugar, and stir well. Pour over rice mixture and stir.

Place rice mixture in a large pan and heat through, turning and mixing. Serve hot, with slivered almonds sprinkled on top.

Serves 6-8

RICE CHOWDER

1 1-lb. chicken, boned and sliced
4 chicken livers
½ cup flour
½ cup peanut oil
1 qt. hot chicken consommé
1 Tbs. soy sauce
1 Tbs. dry sherry
2 cups cooked rice (see p. 73)
¼ cup sliced ginger
3 scallions (whites and 3″ of greens), minced
4 eggs

Bake the chicken in a 375° oven for 10 minutes. While chicken is baking, dredge the chicken livers in flour and fry in the peanut oil until golden. Drain and reserve.

Pour the hot consommé into 4 heat-resistant bowls. Divide the chicken pieces into the bowls with the consommé, cover and bake for 5 minutes. Remove, add soy sauce and sherry and divide the rice into the bowls. Cover and bake for 5 minutes more.

Remove bowls, add ginger and sprinkle with scallions. Drop an egg in each bowl, cover and return to oven for 2 minutes or until egg sets. Serve hot, garnished with one chicken liver per bowl.

Serves 4

RICE WITH SWEET BRANDIED CHESTNUTS

1 4″-square seaweed cake
2 cups Japanese rice
¼ cup mochigome
2 cups water
1 tsp. salt
1 Tbs. sake
½ cup marsala wine
2 Tbs. mirin
1 tsp. soy sauce
¼ cup prepared brandied chestnuts*
Toasted sesame seeds for garnish

Clean the seaweed with a damp cloth and cut into ½″ layers. Combine the Japanese rice and mochigome, wash well and drain.

Bring the rice mixture to a boil with the water and cook at a simmer in a covered pot with the seaweed, salt and sake until rice is tender. Remove seaweed and discard.

Add the marsala, mirin and soy sauce. Stir, bring to a slow simmer, cover and steam for about 5 minutes. Cook for 15 minutes more over a low flame. Remove cover and stir well with a wooden spoon.

Place a cheesecloth over the rice and replace the cover tightly. Let stand for 15 minutes. Put the rice in a bowl, add the brandied chestnuts and mix. Serve sprinkled with sesame seeds.

Serves 4-6

*You can substitute raw chestnuts for the brandied chestnuts. Score the chestnuts with a sharp knife, peel back the skin on one side and toast in the oven until soft. Remove from shells and cut into pieces.

SALMON RICE CAKES

1 cup rice
1½ cups dashi
Salt to taste
1 2½–3-lb. salmon fillet, skinned on one side
½ cup flaked dried bonito
1 sheet of dried seaweed
3 cooked or canned plums, pitted and cut into small pieces
4 oz. red salmon caviar

Bring the rice to a boil in the dashi, lower to a simmer, cover and cook until rice is soft, about 40 minutes.

Salt salmon and keep in a cool place until ready to prepare. Then wash, drain and pat dry. Place on a broiling pan skin side down and broil about 10 minutes. Remove from broiler, skin and cut into ½" cubes. Sprinkle with dried bonito.

Toast the seaweed for a few seconds, then cut into 2½" squares with a pair of scissors. Place 1 Tbs. of rice on half the seaweed squares, flatten and put a salmon cube in the middle. Cover with remaining seaweed squares.

Arrange the rice cakes on a platter with the remaining salmon and the plums and red caviar.

Serves 6

RICE WITH RED AZUKI BEANS

2 cups cooked rice (see p. 73; substitute dashi for water)
1 cup cooked red azuki beans
2 Tbs. chopped, toasted sesame seeds

Sauce:
2 Tbs. soy sauce
1 Tbs. dry sake
1 Tbs. plum wine

Mix the rice well with the red beans. Divide the mixture into individual serving bowls and top with sesame seeds.

Blend the sauce ingredients thoroughly and pour sauce over the rice and beans. Serve.

This dish is a favorite for holidays and special occasions, such as the Emperor's birthday.

Serves 4-6

CHA-ZUKE

2½ cups Japanese boiled rice (see p. 73)
1 cup cubed cooked chicken
12 thin slices of raw fish fillet (white fish of your choice)
6 thin salmon fillets, sautéed in sesame oil
2 Tbs. toasted sesame seeds
6 seaweed leaves
12 tempura shrimp
1½ cups hot green tea

Mix the rice with the chicken cubes and the slices of raw fish and salmon. Sprinkle with sesame seeds and divide into individual bowls.

Cover the rice mixture in each bowl with a seaweed leaf and two shrimp. Pour green tea over each serving. Serve with additional hot green tea.

Serves 6

5
Japanese Specialties

This chapter contains recipes for a number of popular and distinctively Japanese dishes: tempura, sukiyaki, teriyaki, sashimi and oyako-donburi. There are many variations on these dishes, of course, and you should feel free to experiment.

Sauces play a very important role in Japanese cuisine. Some are for dipping, while others are poured over the dish or added during preparation. Soy sauce, sake and sherry (optional) are the principal ingredients in most Japanese sauces, but again there are infinite variations.

Here and throughout this book I have included full information on just the right sauce to complement each dish. But as you become familiar with the tastes and accents of Japanese cuisine, you will want to try your own concoctions.

Tempura

Tempura is perhaps the easiest and most eye-appealing of Japanese dishes. It consists of shrimp, fish, meats and vegetables dipped in a light batter, fried in deep, hot oil until lightly golden and served crisp at once, accompanied by sauces for dipping.

Color plays an important role in tempura cooking, as in Japanese cuisine generally. In planning a tempura meal, choose a wide variety of ingredients and remember to keep the batter coating thin so that their colors will show through. Translucent items are particularly attractive and will add excitement to your selection.

Almost any food can be prepared tempura style. Try a seafood assortment using shrimp (shelled but with tails left on for ease in eating) and fillets of small fish such as trout, smelt, perch and porgy. Or you may want to use chicken or pork. Always include at least six different vegetables. Large white mushrooms with small stems, strips of carrot, eggplant (with skin) and red and green peppers, onion rings, stringbeans, scallions, snow pea pods, water chestnuts and bamboo shoots all make attractive choices.

Tempura ingredients should be fried in vegetable oil, peanut oil or sesame oil heated to 350°. A combination of 75% vegetable or peanut oil and 25% sesame oil gives excellent results, and you will find that the sesame oil imparts a distinctive flavor.

Each kind of ingredient should be fried separately, drained and served immediately to insure crispness. Skim the oil after each frying, adding more if necessary. Special tempura pans are available in houseware departments, fine hardware stores and gourmet shops, but a deep skillet will work just as well.

Preparing tempura for six or more takes a bit of time but is well worth the effort. You will receive compliments galore for this rich symphony of colors and tastes.

TEMPURA BATTER

1½ cups flour sifted
  with ½ cup cornstarch
1 egg, separated
¼ tsp. salt
⅛ tsp. black pepper
1½ cups cold water

Place the flour and cornstarch in a mixing bowl. Beat the egg yolk lightly and add to the flour, mixing well. Stir in salt and pepper. Add water and stir until smooth. Beat the egg white until stiff and fold into the batter.

TEMPURA SAUCE

1 cup dashi or chicken broth
¼ cup soy sauce
¼ cup mirin
1 Tbs. sweet sherry (optional)
1 Tbs. sugar
½ tsp. grated ginger

Combine all the ingredients in a saucepan and bring to a boil. Reduce heat and simmer for 5 minutes. Serve in small dipping bowls.

SWEET AND SPICY TEMPURA SAUCE

¼ cup mirin
1 Tbs. marsala
2 Tbs. orange marmalade
1 tsp. ginger juice
½ tsp. salt
1 Tbs. sugar

Combine all the ingredients in a saucepan and bring to a boil. Reduce heat and simmer for 5 minutes. Serve in small dipping bowls.

Teriyaki

Teriyaki is Japan's closest approximation to shish-kebab. It consists of marinated meat or shellfish skewered on a sharp stick or sword and grilled over a fire or in a broiler. The trick lies in the glaze that is achieved during grilling. Teriyaki is a delicious way to prepare all types of foods, including vegetables.

CHICKEN TERIYAKI WITH LIVERS AND VEGETABLES

1 lb. chicken thighs
1 lb. chicken livers, cleaned and dried
½ lb. fresh mushrooms with ½″ of stem, sliced
½ lb. small white onions
½ lb. cherry tomatoes
8 scallion whites, sliced

Marinade/Glaze:
¼ cup soy sauce
¼ cup sweet sake
1 Tbs. dry sherry (optional)
1 tsp. white sugar
1 tsp. brown sugar
Dash of ginger juice

Prepare the marinade first. Combine the soy sauce, sake, sherry, white sugar and brown sugar and mix with a wire whisk. Add ginger juice and beat slightly. Add the chicken, chicken livers and mushrooms and marinate for 20 minutes.

Thread the chicken, livers, mushrooms, onions, tomatoes and scallions alternately onto bamboo skewers. Brush with marinade and grill over a charcoal fire or in a broiler. Keep turning the skewers and brushing with the marinade.

Grill for about 10 minutes or until well browned and glazed. Serve hot on the skewers.

Serves 4-6

PORK TERIYAKI WITH GINGER GLAZE

1 lb. lean pork,
cut into 2¼″ cubes

3 scallion whites, sliced

Marinade/Glaze:

1/3 cup soy sauce
1/3 cup mirin
1 Tbs. sugar
1 Tbs. apricot preserves
1 Tbs. grated ginger

Prepare the marinade first. Combine all the ingredients in a saucepan and heat to just under a boil. Pour into a bowl and marinate the pork cubes for ½ hour.

Thread the pork cubes and scallion slices alternately onto skewers. Grill until pork is tender and done, turning often and brushing with the marinade to glaze.

Serves 4

Sukiyaki

Sukiyaki is an internationally famous beef and vegetable casserole cooked right on the dinner table in a cast-iron pot and served immediately. For years this culinary delight has been one of the most popular offerings of Japanese restaurants in the United States. Along with tempura, sukiyaki is chiefly responsible for winning converts to Japanese cuisine. Little wonder, for it is a gourmet adventure in taste, eye appeal and appetite fulfillment.

BEEF SUKIYAKI

2 lbs. beef sirloin, filet or tenderloin
1 cup beef bouillon
1 beef bouillon cube
½ cup soy sauce
2 Tbs. sugar
2 Tbs. dry sherry (optional)
1 piece of beef suet
2 bunches of scallions, sliced lengthwise
2 onions, sliced
5 celery stalks, sliced
½ lb. spinach leaves, washed and dried
6 dried black mushrooms, soaked in water, squeezed dry and sliced
1 bean curd cake
1/3 cup shirataki vermicelli

Slice the beef into thin strips 1½" wide and 2" long.

Heat the beef bouillon and add the bouillon cube, stirring to dissolve. Add the soy sauce, sugar and sherry and stir. Bring to a boil and remove from stove.

Melt the suet in a cast-iron pot, add the bouillon broth and vegetables, and simmer. Add the bean curd and vermicelli. Cook uncovered for 5 minutes, stirring. Add the sliced beef and cook until the meat is tender and the vegetables are done, about 15 minutes.

Serves 6-8

Sashimi

Sashimi is a unique Japanese delicacy—raw fish cut or formed into decorative shapes and served with a variety of sauces. All freshwater fish make excellent sashimi, and many saltwater fish are fine too, including sea bass, striped bass, flounder, tuna, bonito, swordfish, mackerel and bluefish.

The first essential in preparing sashimi is that the fish be extremely fresh. To guarantee that the fish is safe to eat raw, you can clean and fillet it, place it in boiling water and quickly transfer it to ice-cold water. Another hygienic method is to leave the skin on one side and place the fish under the broiler for no more than one minute, skin side up. Remove the skin before preparing.

The fish should be cut into small slices or bite-size pieces and arranged on a bed of shredded vegetables, such as lettuce, radish, carrots, and red and white cabbage, along with slivered ginger, watercress and flat parsley. Use your imagination to create attractive and tempting combinations.

Sashimi should be served with a selection of dipping sauces in small bowls. Choose from the recipes below or try your own variations, but always include soy sauce among the ingredients.

SASHIMI SAUCES

Tosa-joyu: Mix ½ cup soy sauce with 1 Tbs. dried bonito flakes and ¼ cup sake. Bring to a boil in a saucepan, remove from heat and serve.

Wasabi-joyu: Blend ½ cup soy sauce with 1 Tbs. Japanese grated horseradish.

Shoga-joyu: Mix ½ cup soy sauce with 1¼ Tbs. ginger juice.

Karashi-joyu: Mix ½ cup soy sauce with ½ tsp. Dijon mustard.

Goma-joyu: In a saucepan mix ½ cup soy sauce, ¼ cup sugar and 2 Tbs. crushed toasted sesame seeds. Heat to just under a boil, remove from heat and strain into dipping bowls.

Kurumi-joyu: Prepare as for goma-joyu, substituting toasted walnuts and almonds for the sesame seeds.

Su-joyu: Mix ¼ cup soy sauce with the juice of 1 lemon.

Sweet sauce: Mix ½ cup soy sauce, 2 Tbs. orange marmalade, 2 Tbs. orange juice, 1½ Tbs. sweet sherry and 1 tsp. sugar. Heat to just under a boil and stir until ingredients are blended and sugar dissolves. Strain into dipping bowls.

SASHIMI OF TROUT

2 trout, skinned and filleted
1 cup shredded radish
1 cup shredded carrots

Sauce:
½ Tbs. powdered or grated Japanese horseradish mixed into a paste with a little water
½ cup soy sauce
1 Tbs. dry sherry
¾ Tbs. sugar

Slice the fish into strips about 2½" long, 1" wide and ¼" thick. Mix together the radish and carrots, divide the mixture equally into 4 small bowls and top with slices of fish.

To prepare the sauce, mix the ingredients together, stirring well to dissolve the sugar. Pour into small dipping bowls and serve with the fish and vegetables.

Serves 4

OYAKO-DONBURI

This is a classic rice dish. The name actually refers to the garnishes over the rice, usually shredded chicken and egg. Beef and pork are also used. Oyako-donburi makes an excellent hot luncheon dish. It should be served in bowls, accompanied by sauce.

5 cups rice
1 large cooked chicken breast, skinned, boned and cut into ¼″ cubes
4 scallions, cut lengthwise and sliced
½ cup sliced mushrooms
8 eggs, beaten lightly
Salt and pepper to taste
1 sheet of seaweed, shredded, for garnish
1 Tbs. chopped parsley for garnish

Sauce:
1 cup dashi
2 Tbs. sake
2 Tbs. sweet sherry
2 tsp. sugar
4 Tbs. soy sauce

Steam the rice until cooked. Place in a heat-resistant bowl in a 225° oven to keep warm.

Combine the sauce ingredients, stir well and pour into a skillet. Heat and cook for about 3 minutes.

Mix the chicken with the scallions and mushrooms, then add the eggs and salt and pepper to taste. Mix well and pour slowly into the skillet with the sauce. Stir and cover, then cook to allow eggs to set, no more than 3 minutes.

Slide the omelette onto a heated platter and cut into 4 equal portions. Place the rice in wide bowls or on plates as a bed for the omelette portions, cover with a small amount of sauce and garnish with seaweed and parsley. Serve any remaining sauce on the side.

Serves 4

6
Fish and Shellfish

Japan is a fish-eating nation. Its rivers and lakes provide many kinds of sweetwater fish, and the surrounding oceans and seas abound with saltwater fish and shellfish.

The cuisine of Japan and Southeast Asia offers a wide array of creative possibilities for the preparation of fish. Some of the choicest are included in this chapter. The preparation of *sashimi,* Japan's unique delicacy—raw fish served in a variety of attractive and delectable ways—is described in Chapter 5, "Japanese Specialties."

STEAMED BASS

½ cup white wine
3 Tbs. sweet sake
4 Tbs. soy sauce
1 Tbs. white vinegar
1 tsp. salt
⅛ tsp. peppercorns
1 tsp. lemon juice
¼ cup water
1 1″ cube of fresh ginger, peeled and thinly sliced
1 3-lb. sea bass or striped bass, cleaned and dried, with head and tail
1 large onion, sliced
6 carrots, sliced lengthwise
3 scallions, thinly sliced, for garnish
½ cup brandied chestnuts for garnish

In the bottom of a fish steamer combine the wine, sake, soy sauce, vinegar, ½ tsp. of salt, peppercorns, lemon juice, water and ginger.

Salt the inside of the fish with the remaining salt. Place the fish in the steamer and marinate for 1–2 hours, turning every half hour. Remove fish and place the rack in the steamer.

Put the fish, onions and carrots on the rack and steam for 20 minutes. Remove fish to a heated platter and take off head and tail. Skin, fillet and slice diagonally.

Divide the fish and vegetables equally onto serving dishes. Garnish with scallions and chestnuts.

Serves 4

BROILED MARINATED MACKEREL

2½ lbs. mackerel fillets, with skin
Salt and pepper to taste
Lemon juice
1 lemon, thinly sliced

Marinade:
½ cup sake
½ Tbs. sugar
½ cup orange juice
½ cup dashi

Prepare the marinade first. Combine all the ingredients in a bowl and stir.

Sprinkle the fillets on both sides with salt, pepper and lemon juice. Soak fillets in the marinade for 1 hour with half the lemon slices, turning and mixing every 15 minutes.

Remove fillets from marinade, place on a grill and broil for 6 minutes on each side, brushing with marinade several times. Remove from broiler, slice and brush with remaining marinade.

Place fish on a platter over thinly shredded lettuce or cabbage and serve garnished with remaining lemon slices.

Serves 4

SALMON IN TEA SAUCE

1 large can of salmon
¼ cup sake
¼ cup soy sauce
2 cups Japanese boiled rice (see p. 73)
¼ cup toasted chopped sesame seeds
1 cup hot green tea

Remove any skin or bones from the salmon and place in a saucepan with the sake and soy sauce. Simmer until liquid is almost absorbed.

Place the rice in individual bowls, top with the salmon, sprinkle with sesame seeds and add tea. Cover the bowls and let stand for 2 minutes. Serve hot.

Serves 4

SALMON STEAK WITH MARINATED MUSHROOMS

4 fresh salmon steaks, washed and patted dry
2 Tbs. flour
2 Tbs. corn oil
Lemon juice

Salmon Marinade:
3 Tbs. soy sauce
2 Tbs. sake
1 tsp. grated ginger
2 leeks, finely chopped

Marinated Mushrooms:
1 pt. fresh white mushrooms, washed, trimmed and sliced
½ cup white wine vinegar
1 Tbs. soy sauce
¼ tsp. dill weed
⅛ tsp. each salt and pepper

Prepare the mushrooms first. Place mushrooms in a sauce made of the remaining ingredients, cover and refrigerate for 2 hours or more.

To prepare the salmon marinade, thoroughly mix all the ingredients, using chopsticks. Add the salmon steaks, cover and refrigerate for at least 1 hour, turning occasionally.

Drain the fish and sprinkle on both sides with flour. Heat the corn oil in a large skillet and cook the fish over moderate heat until both sides are golden brown.

Serve the fish hot, sprinkled with a little lemon juice, and accompanied by the strained marinated mushrooms and some chopped lettuce and shredded cabbage.

Serves 4

FISH WITH RED MISO

1 cup dashi
2 Tbs. sugar
¼ cup sake
Salt and pepper to taste
1 1″ piece of ginger, thinly sliced
4 fillets of mackerel, whitefish or snapper, thinly sliced
¼ cup red miso
2 scallion whites, thinly sliced, for garnish

Mix the dashi, sugar, sake, salt, pepper and ginger in a saucepan. Stir, bring to a boil, lower heat and add fish. Cover and cook over a low flame for 5 minutes.

Mix the miso with a small amount of broth from the saucepan to make a smooth paste. Add to the saucepan and stir well. Return mixture to a boil, lower heat and simmer, covered, for 10–15 minutes longer.

Arrange the fish on serving dishes, cover with sauce and garnish with scallions.

Serves 4

FISH-STUFFED CABBAGE

4 large cabbage leaves*
2 lbs. ground fillet of flounder, whitefish or whiting
2 Tbs. sake
1½ Tbs. sherry
2½ Tbs. cornstarch
¼ tsp. salt
⅛ tsp. white pepper
2 Tbs. chopped flat parsley
Vegetable oil for frying
4 Tbs. mustard for garnish
4 lemon slices for garnish

Sauce:

1 Tbs. Japanese rice vinegar or wine vinegar
3 Tbs. soy sauce
2 Tbs. sherry (optional)

Rinse the cabbage leaves, drain and pat dry.

Mix the ground fish with the sake, sherry, 1½ Tbs. of the cornstarch, salt, pepper and parsley. Sprinkle the cabbage leaves with the remaining cornstarch. Divide the fish mixture equally onto the cabbage leaves, roll and secure ends tightly.

Cover the bottom of a saucepan with vegetable oil and fry the cabbage rolls for 10–12 minutes until brown on both sides, turning once. Remove to paper toweling to drain.

Prepare the sauce by beating the ingredients with chopsticks or a wire whisk. Pour into 4 small bowls for dipping.

Place the cabbage rolls on individual plates, slice and serve at room temperature with a dab of mustard and a lemon slice.

Serves 4

*You can substitute green peppers or spinach leaves for the cabbage leaves.

FISH FILLET WITH BEAN CURD AND MUSHROOMS

1 lb. fillet of sole
  or flounder
½ lb. bean curd
½ pt. fresh mushrooms
A few Tbs. flour
¼ cup peanut oil

Hot Sauce:
1 cup chicken broth
¼ cup soy sauce
½ Tbs. sugar
1½ Tbs. mirin

Cut the fillet into long strips, then cut again diagonally into smaller pieces. Roll the bean curd in a cloth and press to remove moisture. Cut into 1″ cubes. Trim the mushroom stems close to the caps.

Sprinkle the fish pieces, curd cubes and mushrooms with flour. Heat the oil in a heavy skillet. Fry fish until golden brown and remove to a heated platter. Fry bean curd until golden and remove to a bowl with a slotted spoon. Fry mushrooms until golden, about 3 minutes, turning a few times. Remove to a heated dish to drain on paper toweling.

To make the hot sauce, put the chicken broth in a saucepan and add remaining ingredients. Mix well and bring to a boil. Remove from heat.

Place the fish, curd and mushrooms in separate bowls. Pour hot sauce over each bowl and serve with green salad and hot rice.

Serves 4

STUFFED BROILED FISH

3 eggs, beaten
¾ cup chopped snow peas
½ cup minced mushroom caps
Vegetable oil
Salt and pepper to taste
3 large trout, bass, pickerel or fish of your choice, cleaned and slit on one side
9 raw bacon strips

Scramble the eggs with the snow peas and mushrooms in an oiled pan until soft. Add salt and pepper.

Fill the fish cavities with the egg mixture. Wrap 3 strips of bacon around each fish and secure with toothpicks. Broil fish for 5 minutes on each side.

Serves 4-6

STEAMED FISH DUMPLINGS

2 lbs. ground fillet of flounder
½ cup chopped onion
¼ cup chopped carrots
4 dried black mushrooms, soaked, drained and chopped
1 Tbs. sugar
½ Tbs. minced ginger
¼ tsp. salt
1 egg white, stiffly beaten
1 cup raw rice, soaked for 2 hours and drained
1 clove garlic, finely chopped
½ cup soy sauce

Thoroughly mix the fish with the onions, carrots, mushrooms, sugar, ginger, salt and egg white. Form the mixture into small balls about the size of ping-pong balls and roll in rice, pressing to cover completely.

Place fish balls in a steamer, cover and steam for 20–30 minutes. Mix the garlic with the soy sauce, heat and serve over the hot dumplings.

Serves 4

FISH FRITTERS

2–3 lbs. fillet (fish of your choice), chopped
½ cup chopped scallions
2 carrots, finely chopped
½ tsp. chopped ginger
2 Tbs. miso
1 tsp. soy sauce
2 egg whites, stiffly beaten
4 tsp. cornstarch
Peanut oil for frying

Sauce:
1 tsp. soy sauce
1 tsp. sake
1 tsp. lemon juice

Thoroughly blend the fish with the remaining ingredients except the egg whites, cornstarch and oil. Then add egg whites and mix again, slowly. Form the fish mixture into round patties and sprinkle with cornstarch.

Cover the bottom of a skillet with peanut oil, heat and fry the patties on both sides until crisp and golden. Remove to paper toweling to drain.

Drain the oil from the skillet until only 2 Tbs. remain. Return patties to skillet, cover and simmer for 5 minutes to steam.

To make the sauce, thoroughly combine all the ingredients. Serve to accompany the hot fish fritters.

Serves 4

SHRIMP WITH BRUSSELS SPROUTS

1 lb. medium-size shrimp or prawns, shelled, cleaned and split, with tails intact

1 lb. Brussels sprouts

Soy sauce

4 lemon wedges for garnish

Sauce:

4 Tbs. white wine vinegar

1 Tbs. soy sauce

Cook the split shrimp in salted boiling water for 3 minutes. Drain and remove to a heated dish.

Trim the bases of the Brussels sprouts and score with a sharp knife. Boil sprouts in salted water until tender. Drain and put a little soy sauce in the scored bases.

Place shrimp on a bed of shredded lettuce, surround with sprouts and garnish with lemon wedges.

Prepare the sauce by mixing the vinegar and soy sauce. Serve in small dishes for dipping.

Serves 4

SHRIMP AND CUSTARD WITH COLD SAUCE

6 eggs, lightly beaten
½ cup dashi
½ Tbs. soy sauce
18 shrimp, shelled, cleaned, cooked and chilled
1 cup small green peas, cooked, drained and chilled
Chopped scallions for garnish

Cold Sauce:
½ cup dashi
1 tsp. soy sauce
½ tsp. sugar
1 tsp. cornstarch mixed with 2 Tbs. dashi

Blend the eggs, dashi and soy sauce. Pour into 6 heat-resistant custard cups and steam for about 15 minutes, or until custard sets. Allow to cool and place in refrigerator to chill.

To make the sauce, combine dashi, soy sauce and sugar in a saucepan. Add cornstarch mixture and stir well. Bring to a boil, stir, remove from heat and allow to cool. Place in refrigerator to chill.

To serve, place 3 shrimp and some peas in each custard cup and spoon on the chilled sauce. Garnish with chopped scallions.

Serves 6

CRAYFISH IN SAUCE

½ cup sake
¼ cup water
2 lbs. crayfish or shrimp, shelled and cleaned, with tails
¼ cup soy sauce
¼ cup dry sherry
1 Tbs. sugar

In a saucepan bring the sake and water to a boil, add the crayfish and cook for 1 minute. Add the soy sauce and sherry, stir in the sugar and cook for 4 minutes.

Serve the crayfish in a bowl with the sauce poured over.

Serves 4

DEEP-FRIED OYSTERS OR CLAMS

2 dozen oysters or large clams, shelled, washed and drained
¼ tsp. salt
½ tsp. sugar
1 dried hot red pepper, seeded, trimmed and chopped
¼ cup sake
¼ cup dry sherry
½ lb. stringbeans
1 cup water
¼ cup peanut oil for frying
1 1" piece of white radish, grated
Soy sauce for dipping

Batter:
2 eggs, beaten
¾ cup white cake flour
2 Tbs. sake
1 sheet of seaweed, toasted and crumbled

Marinate the fish in a mixture of the salt, sugar, red pepper, sake and sherry for 1 hour.

Boil the stringbeans in the water for 5 minutes. Drain and dry.

Prepare the batter by combining all the ingredients and mixing until smooth.

Heat the oil until very hot. Dip the stringbeans in batter and fry until golden. Drain. Dip the oysters in batter and fry until golden. Drain. Serve at once with grated radish and soy sauce.

Serves 4

BAKED CLAMS IN SALT SHELLS

1 dozen large cherrystone clams
2 egg whites, stiffly beaten
Coarse salt
½ Tbs. sake
Lemon slices for garnish

Preheat oven to 425°.

Slit the muscle that holds the clam to the shell, but leave shells unopened. Brush both halves of the shell with egg white and dip in the coarse salt until shells are covered all over with a thick layer of salt.

Bake the clams for 5–10 minutes, depending on size. Remove from oven, open the shells slightly and add a little sake to the inside, then close the shells. Serve hot with lemon slices.

Serves 3–4

FRIED OYSTERS GARNISHED WITH SPINACH

2 dozen oysters, shucked, washed and drained
1 Tbs. sake
1 Tbs. soy sauce
⅛ tsp. salt
⅛ tsp. Japanese pepper
½ cup flour
¼ cup peanut oil or vegetable oil
2 eggs, beaten lightly
2 cups cooked spinach

Marinate the oysters in the sake, soy sauce, salt and pepper for 15 minutes. Drain oysters and roll in flour.

Heat the oil in a skillet. Dip floured oysters in the egg and fry until lightly brown all over.

Drain and serve hot with the heated spinach.

Serves 6

WHITE FISH WITH RICE

1 1½–2-lb. white fish (your choice), boned and cleaned
1¾ cups water (more if needed
2 onions, sliced
1¼ tsp. salt
¼ tsp. pepper
2/3 cup raw rice, washed
4 Tbs. butter
1 large onion, chopped
1 clove garlic, minced
¾ tsp. turmeric
2 hard-boiled eggs, sliced, for garnish
Dried chili peppers for garnish
3 pimientos, sliced, for garnish

Place fish in a pan with enough water to cover. Add onion slices, 1 tsp. of the salt, and the pepper. Boil over moderate heat for 15 minutes, or until fish is tender. Remove onion slices with a slotted spoon and discard. Remove fish and shred.

Bring water in pan to a second boil, add the remaining ¼ tsp. salt and the rice, cover and simmer for 10–15 minutes until rice is soft.

Heat the butter in a skillet. Add chopped onion and garlic and sauté for 5 minutes until onion is golden. Add turmeric and cook for 1 more minute. Add shredded fish and cooked rice and stir. Simmer for 3 minutes.

Serve on a large platter garnished with the eggs, chili peppers and pimientos.

Serves 4

SOLE CROQUETTES

1/3 cup peanut oil
1 tsp. salt
½ tsp. turmeric
1 tsp. grated lemon rind
3 cloves garlic, minced
2 onions, chopped
1/3 tsp. ground chili pepper
1½ lbs. ground fillet of sole
⅛ cup flour
2 large tomatoes, minced

Heat half the oil in a large skillet and add the salt, turmeric, lemon rind, garlic, onions and chili pepper. Sauté for 8 minutes, stirring. Add half of this mixture to the fish, blend well and form patties. Sprinkle with flour.

Heat the remaining oil in the pan with the other half of the onion-seasoning mixture. Add the fish and brown on both sides. Add the tomatoes and cook for 15 minutes. Serve hot with rice.

Serves 2-3

FISH WITH TOMATOES

1 2-lb. bass, snapper
  or any saltwater fish
1 tsp. turmeric
¼ cup vegetable or peanut oil
¼ cup butter
2 onions, sliced
2 cloves garlic, minced
¼ tsp. ground ginger
Salt and pepper to taste
1 lb. tomatoes, sliced
1½ tsp. lemon juice

Clean, skin and wash the fish and slice it into serving pieces. Rub all over with turmeric and oil, reserving 1 tsp. of the oil. Melt and brown the butter with the onions and fish, turning often.

Pound the garlic and ginger to a paste with the tsp. of oil. Spoon the paste onto the fish, add salt and pepper and cook for another 5 minutes. Place the tomato slices over the fish, cover and cook for 10 minutes more. Sprinkle with lemon juice and serve.

Serves 4

FRIED SMELTS

2 lbs. smelts, cleaned, heads removed

2 cups vegetable oil for frying

Marinade:

6 Tbs. soy sauce
6 Tbs. sherry
2 Tbs. sugar
½ tsp. coriander
1 tsp. Chinese spices
1 tsp. ground ginger
2 scallions, chopped
1 Tbs. vinegar

Prepare the marinade first by combining all the ingredients in a large bowl. Place the fish in the marinade, cover and chill for 1 hour or more, turning every 15 minutes.

Drain the fish and pat dry. Heat the oil in a wok or large skillet and fry the fish until brown and crisp, turning once. Drain on paper toweling and serve hot.

Serves 4-6

STEAMED BASS

1 2½-lb. sea bass, cleaned, with head
1 tsp. salt
¼ cup honey
4 Tbs. soy sauce
2 Tbs. sherry
8 dried black mushrooms, soaked in water for 10 minutes and drained
2 1" pieces of ginger, thinly sliced
6 scallions, cut into ½" rounds
1 cup water

Rub the fish thoroughly with the salt, honey, soy sauce and sherry. Allow to marinate for 20 minutes, turning once. Drain fish and reserve marinade.

Place the fish in an ovenproof dish, then place the dish on a rack in a roasting pan. Put the marinade, mushrooms, ginger and scallions over the fish and pour the water into the bottom of the roasting pan. Cover and steam for 30–35 minutes or until soft. Serve with rice.

Serves 4

SOLE IN WINE SAUCE

1½ lbs. fillet of sole, sliced
1 egg white, stiffly beaten
A few Tbs. cornstarch
¼ cup cooking oil for frying
5 Tbs. sherry
1½ Tbs. cornstarch dissolved in 8 Tbs. chicken bouillon
¼ cup honey

Dip the fish slices in the egg white and sprinkle with cornstarch. In a heavy skillet brown the fish in the oil on both sides. Remove and drain.

Add to the skillet the sherry, cornstarch mixture and honey. Stir over moderate heat until thick. Return fish to skillet, cover with sauce, heat through and serve.

Serves 2

TOASTED FISH

4 slices of white bread
1½ lbs. fillet of sole
2 eggs, beaten
with salt and pepper
4 slices of bread, toasted and
crumbled into breadcrumbs
Vegetable oil for frying
Parsley sprigs for garnish

Trim the crusts from the slices of white bread and cut each slice into quarters. Cut the fish into pieces to fit on the bread quarters.

Dip the fish pieces in the egg, then dip the bread pieces in the egg. Place the fish on the bread and coat well with breadcrumbs.

Fry the fish toasts in hot oil for 3 minutes on each side or until brown. Serve garnished with parsley.

Serves 2-3

LOBSTER IN EGG SAUCE

2 1-1½-lb. lobsters,
shelled and cleaned
2 cloves garlic, minced
2 scallions, chopped
½ cup vegetable oil
1¼ cups finely diced pork
5 Tbs. soy sauce
1 tsp. ground ginger or 2 slices
of fresh ginger, ground
1½ Tbs. cornstarch
2/3 cup chicken consommé
3 Tbs. sherry
1 Tbs. sugar
3 eggs, beaten
1/3 cup water

Cut the lobster meat, including the meat from the claws, into 2″ pieces. Fry the garlic and scallions in the oil for 2 minutes, then add the pork and stir-fry for 4 minutes. Add the lobster pieces and fry for 3 minutes more, then stir in 4 Tbs. of the soy sauce and the ginger.

Mix the cornstarch with the consommé, sherry and sugar. Add to the lobster mixture. Mix the beaten eggs with the remaining Tbs. of soy sauce and the water and stir into the lobster mixture. Lower the heat and simmer for 5 minutes. Serve at once.

Serves 4-6

SHRIMP AND VEGETABLES

1 large onion, chopped
2 cloves garlic, chopped
¾ tsp. each cumin, coriander, ginger and salt
1/3 tsp. ground chili pepper
1 Tbs. peanut oil
1 cup coconut milk
2 carrots, minced
1 cup frozen peas
1 cup minced stringbeans
1 cup shredded cabbage
1 celery stalk, minced
1 Tbs. grated lemon rind
1½ lbs. shrimp, shelled cleaned and cubed

Sauté the onion, garlic, seasonings and chili pepper in the hot oil for 5 minutes, stirring. Slowly add the coconut milk, heat and stir in the vegetables and lemon rind. Cook slowly, covered, for ½ hour, then add the shrimp and cook for another 10 minutes.

Serves 4-6

BAKED FISH

1 Tbs. vegetable oil
Salt and pepper to taste
1 clove garlic, minced
1 3-lb. fish of your choice, sliced in half and boned
4 Tbs. melted butter
¼ tsp. ground chili pepper
3 Tbs. soy sauce
6 tsp. lemon juice

Preheat oven to 375°.

Mash the oil, salt, pepper and garlic into a paste. Rub the fish all over with the paste and place in an oiled baking dish.

Combine the butter, chili pepper, soy sauce and lemon juice. Cover the fish with this mixture and bake for 30 minutes, basting often. Serve hot with rice.

Serves 4

CRAB AND SHRIMP RICE

¼ cup vegetable oil
2 onions, chopped
2 cloves garlic, chopped
2 cups cooked rice
1 lb. shrimp, shelled and cleaned
1 8-oz. can of crab meat, chopped
1½ cups sliced ham
1 tsp. coriander
¾ tsp. cumin
1/3 tsp. chili pepper
¼ tsp. mace
3 Tbs. peanut butter
1 hard-boiled egg, thinly sliced, for garnish

Heat the oil in a skillet and sauté the onions and garlic until golden. Stir in the rice and cook for 5 minutes, or until browned. If necessary, add more oil.

Add the shrimp, crab meat, ham, seasonings and peanut butter to the skillet. Sauté for 10 more minutes, stirring. Serve hot garnished with egg slices.

This dish is delicious accompanied by chopped cucumbers, tomatoes, chutney, relish, peanuts and bananas.

Serves 4

SPICY FRIED FISH

¾ cup flour
¼ tsp. salt
2 Tbs. olive oil
¾ cup water
4 small fillets of flounder or any white fish
¼ lb. mushrooms, chopped
6 Tbs. vinegar
1 large onion or 2 scallion whites, chopped
2 Tbs. sugar
2 tomatoes, chopped
2 Tbs. soy sauce
¼ cup fresh minced ginger or 2 Tbs. ground ginger
1 Tbs. cornstarch
Chopped parsley for garnish
Lemon slices for garnish

Make a paste of the flour, salt, olive oil and half the water. Cover the fillets thoroughly with the paste and fry in a little more olive oil until crisp and brown on both sides. Remove to a heated platter.

In a saucepan combine the mushrooms, vinegar, onions, sugar, tomatoes, soy sauce and ginger and simmer for 10 minutes. Blend the cornstarch with the remaining water and add to the saucepan. Stir, bring to a boil, lower heat and cook slowly for 5 minutes.

Cover the fish with parsley and lemon slices. Pour the sauce over the fish and serve hot.

Serves 4

BROILED SHRIMP

1 Tbs. coriander
¼ tsp. ground chili pepper
1 tsp. turmeric
½ tsp. salt
4 small onions, quartered, then sliced
3 garlic cloves, sliced
½ cup melted butter
1 lb. shrimp, shelled and cleaned

Combine all the ingredients with the melted butter and marinate the shrimp in the mixture for at least 1 hour, turning often. Remove shrimp and reserve marinade.

Place shrimp on a broiling pan and broil for 4 minutes on each side until tender but not overcooked. Serve hot, with the marinade on the side.

Serves 2

7
Meat and Poultry

Meat and poultry dishes are relatively recent additions to the cuisine of Japan, having come into popularity only after Commodore Perry's visit in the 1850s. But these Western culinary staples are now favorites with the Japanese, though often different from what Americans are used to in appearance and style of preparation. For one thing, meat and poultry are usually cut up, shredded or sliced to make eating with chopsticks easier.

Today the cattle of Kobe, Japan, are considered to provide the finest beef available anywhere in the world. Unusually well fed and well cared for, they are rubbed down by hand to help distribute their fat. During the last part of their lives, they are hand-fed Kirin beer to soften the meat and make it tender.

Most gourmets agree that Japanese cooking is extraordinary for its attractiveness and simplicity of preparation. Japan's meat and poultry dishes are no exception. They are exquisite and elegant examples of *haute cuisine.* This chapter contains some of the best Japanese meat and poultry recipes, along with a sampling of dishes from Burma, China, Hong Kong, Indonesia and Thailand.

FRIED PORK

1 lb. loin of pork, boned and trimmed
1 Tbs. vegetable oil mixed with 1 Tbs. sesame oil
A few dashes of Japanese pepper
A few dashes of soy sauce

Cover the meat with the mixed oils and fry over moderate heat for 20 minutes, or until meat is tender. Remove meat and drain.

Cut into bite-size pieces, sprinkle with pepper and soy sauce, and serve hot.

Serves 4

PORK OVER GRATED RADISH

1 Tbs. vegetable oil
1 lb. pork, boned, trimmed and cut into ½″ cubes
¼ cup sake
¼ cup soy sauce
1½ cups grated horseradish

Heat the oil in a heavy skillet and sauté the pork, adding the sake and soy sauce. Stir frequently. Cook uncovered over moderate heat for 10 minutes or until browned on all sides.

Place the grated horseradish on a serving dish, top with the meat, and pour the sauce from the skillet into a dipping bowl. Serve with Japanese boiled rice (see p. 73).

Serves 4

SESAME PORK IN MUSTARD SAUCE

1/3 cup sesame seeds
1½ lbs. pork, sliced
¼ cup dry sherry
¼ cup soy sauce
1¼ Tbs. dry mustard mixed with enough water to make a paste
1 Tbs. sugar
Sliced scallions for garnish

Parch the sesame seeds in a hot frying pan until they jump. Remove from pan and chop.

Brown the pork on all sides in an oiled skillet. Pour the sherry and soy sauce over the meat and stir. Add the mustard paste and sugar and stir until well mixed. Add the sesame seeds and stir.

Cook at a moderate pace for 5 minutes or until pork is done. Arrange pork on a platter, pour sauce over it and garnish with scallions.

Serves 4

PORK WITH ASSORTED VEGETABLES

1 lb. loin of pork, cut into slices 4″ square and 1″ thick
Salt and pepper
½ cup flour
1 egg, beaten
¼ cup sesame oil mixed with ½ cup vegetable oil
¼ lb. sliced ham
1 cup chopped bamboo shoots
4 dried black mushrooms, soaked, squeezed dry and chopped
1 cucumber, peeled and cubed
1 tomato, cubed
¼ cup ketchup
3 Tbs. sugar
1 Tbs. wine vinegar
1 Tbs. sherry
1 tsp. cornstarch

Sprinkle the pork slices with salt and pepper and pat all over with flour. Dip in beaten egg and fry in hot oil to cover until brown. Drain on paper toweling. Cut pork slices in half diagonally.

In a separate pan sauté the ham and all the vegetables for a few minutes in the remainder of the oil, stirring all the time. Add the ketchup, sugar, vinegar, sherry and cornstarch. Stir.

Arrange the meat in a circle around the rim of a large platter. Fill the center with the vegetables and garnish with sauce from the pan.

Serves 4

PORK WITH SESAME GARNISH

1½ lbs. pork, sliced into strips 3″ long and 1″ thick
3 Tbs. soy sauce
1 tsp. ginger juice
3 Tbs. peanut oil
Cucumber slices for garnish

Sesame Paste:
1 tsp. soy sauce
2 Tbs. sake
1 Tbs. sugar
½ cup dry sherry
1 tsp. cornstarch
2½ Tbs. parched ground sesame seeds

Marinate the pork strips in the soy sauce and ginger juice for ½ hour. Heat the oil and sauté the pork until browned on all sides. Remove and drain. Keep warm on a heated platter.

To make the sesame paste, combine soy sauce, sake, sugar and sherry in a saucepan. Heat to a simmer and stir. Add cornstarch and stir well to dissolve and smooth. Add sesame seeds and stir well. Cook over moderate heat until mixture thickens and forms a paste.

Spread the sesame paste on the pork strips, arrange on a platter and garnish with cucumber slices.

Serves 2

GLAZED PORK BALLS

1 lb. ground pork
3 scallion whites, chopped
½ cup Japanese boiled rice
(see p. 73)
¼ cup chopped water chestnuts
1 egg, lightly beaten
½ Tbs. ginger juice
½ Tbs. sake
3 Tbs. soy sauce
½ Tbs. sugar

In a mixing bowl blend the meat with the scallions, rice, water chestnuts and beaten egg. Form into well-packed balls.

Combine the ginger juice and sake with half the soy sauce. Mix well. Marinate the pork balls in this mixture for ½ hour, turning and basting every 10 minutes.

In a large oiled skillet sauté the pork balls to brown on all sides, for about 25 minutes or until done. Remove to a hot platter.

Add the sugar and the remaining soy sauce to the marinade, then bring to a simmer in a small pot. Add pork balls and cook over a high flame for 3 minutes to glaze. Remove and serve with salad.

Serves 3

DEEP-FRIED PORK

2½ lbs. boneless loin of pork, cut into slices ¼″ thick
3 Tbs. soy sauce
3 Tbs. sherry
1 Tbs. sugar
1 egg white, beaten
Cornstarch to coat
1 cup vegetable oil for frying

Sauce:
2 Tbs. sesame oil
¼ tsp. coriander
2 Tbs. sweet sherry
1/3 cup soy sauce
4 Tbs. vinegar
½ cup chicken stock
6 Tbs. sugar

Marinate the pork in the soy sauce, sherry and sugar for at least ½ hour, turning often. Add egg white to the marinade and sprinkle the pork slices with cornstarch. Set aside.

To make the sauce, heat the sesame oil in a saucepan, add coriander and stir. Add the liquids and sugar and bring to a boil, stirring all the time. Cover and turn off heat.

Heat the vegetable oil in a wok and deep-fry the pork slices one by one for 3 minutes or until brown. Drain and serve on a large platter, accompanied by sauce for dipping. Have salt and pepper on the table for seasoning.

Serves 4

SPICED PORK

2 lbs. boneless pork, sliced
4 beets, peeled and sliced
4 carrots, sliced
3 Tbs. ground coriander
½ tsp. black peppercorns
¼ tsp. grated ginger
¼ tsp. salt
4 onions, sliced
¾ cup unsalted butter
½ lb. spinach,
cooked and chopped
3 pickled pimientos, sliced
¼ tsp. saffron mixed with
¼ tsp. lukewarm water
1 cup sugar
Juice of 1 lemon

Put the pork, beets, carrots, coriander, peppercorns, ginger and salt in a large pan, add a little hot water and cook at a simmer until meat is tender, adding more water as needed. Remove meat and reserve gravy.

Brown the onions in the butter. Add meat and brown.

Heat the cooked spinach and pimientos in a pot with the reserved gravy. Add the meat and onions and stir in the saffron mixture. Remove from heat.

Make a syrup of the sugar and lemon juice, add to the pot and stir. Return to moderate heat and cook for 10 minutes. Stir again and serve over rice.

Serves 4-6

SPARERIBS SIMMERED IN SAUCE

2 lbs. spareribs
2 Tbs. dry sherry
4 Tbs. white wine vinegar
2 Tbs. soy sauce
5 Tbs. sugar
¼ cup water

Separate the spareribs and cut each rib into thirds without removing the bone. Place ribs in a deep, heavy skillet over high heat and quickly sear all over.

Add all remaining ingredients, stir and simmer for 45 minutes, covered. Remove cover, stir and turn ribs, and cook until sauce is evaporated. Serve hot with rice.

Serves 6-8

SWEET AND SOUR PORK

2 lbs. pork tenderloin, sliced ¼″ thick
3 Tbs. dry sherry
¾ Tbs. grated ginger
1 Tbs. cornstarch
½ cup peanut oil
1½ cups chunk pineapple
1 cup sliced green pepper
1 cup sliced red pepper
1 celery stalk, sliced
¼ lb. snow peas, sliced
1 scallion white, sliced
2″ of scallion green, minced
¼ cup white wine vinegar
1¼ cups pineapple juice
2 tomatoes, cut into chunks
2 Tbs. cornstarch mixed with ¼ cup water

Egg Batter:
2 eggs, lightly beaten
¾ cup flour
¼ tsp. salt
1/3 cup water

Sauce:
1 tsp. soy sauce
3 Tbs. brown sugar
¼ cup chili sauce
1 tsp. Worcestershire sauce

Marinate the pork in the sherry and ginger for 30 minutes, stirring and turning frequently.

While the pork is marinating, make the egg batter by beating together all the batter ingredients.

Drain the pork slices, dip them into egg batter and sprinkle with cornstarch. Heat some of the peanut oil in a wok and fry pork until golden brown. Remove to a heated platter.

Add a little more oil to the wok. Put the pineapple chunks, peppers, celery, snow peas and scallions in the wok and stir-fry for 3 minutes. Add the vinegar and pineapple juice and cook for 1 minute longer. Add the tomatoes and cook for another minute. Stir in the cornstarch mixture and cook over a high flame for 2 minutes, until mixture thickens.

To make the sauce, combine all sauce ingredients well with 1 Tbs. of the thick sauce from the wok. Stir and bring to a boil in a saucepan. Pour into a bowl and serve with the pork.

Serve the pork and vegetables over rice with a spoonful of sauce from the wok.

Serves 4

BROILED BEEF WITH MISO

1 cup red miso
¼ cup sugar
2 Tbs. dry sherry
1½ lbs. sirloin or round steak
4 pieces of pickled ginger for garnish

In a bowl combine the miso, sugar and sherry to form a smooth paste.

Cut the beef into 4 slices, then score the edges of each slice with a sharp knife. Spread the miso paste on one side of each slice and cover with cheesecloth. Repeat for the other side, again covering with cheesecloth.

Wrap the covered beef slices tightly in aluminum foil and place in the refrigerator for a few hours. Remove from refrigerator, unwrap foil and remove cheesecloth and miso paste.

Broil meat for about 5 minutes on each side, depending on desired rareness. Cut into diagonal slices and arrange on dinner plates, garnished with the ginger pieces.

Serves 2

BRAISED STEAK WITH GARLIC AND GINGER

1 2-lb sirloin steak, ½″ thick
½ clove garlic, mashed
Dash each of salt and white pepper
1 tsp. ginger juice
Peanut oil for braising

Season the steak with the garlic, salt, pepper and ginger juice. Cover the bottom of a large, heavy skillet with peanut oil and heat. Sear steak well on one side.

Add 1 tsp. of oil, turn steak and sear again for about 5 minutes or until pink. Remove from skillet, slice into strips 1″ thick and serve with rice.

Serves 4

JAPANESE BRISKET OF BEEF

3 lbs. brisket of beef, trimmed
1 lb. Japanese white radish
¼ cup peeled diced ginger
¼ tsp. salt

Sauce:
4 Tbs. soy sauce
¼ cup dry sherry
1 cup orange juice

Cut beef into 1″ cubes. Trim radish but do not peel. Cut radish into slices 1″ thick, then cut each slice in half.

Place the beef, radish and ginger in a large saucepan and cover with boiling water. Put a lid on the pan and simmer for 1½ hours or longer. Add salt for the last 15 minutes.

To make the sauce, combine all ingredients in a saucepan, bring to a boil and simmer for 5 minutes. Allow to cool.

Serve the beef hot, accompanied by sauce for dipping.

Serves 4

SCALLION-STUFFED BEEF ROLLS

2 lbs. round steak or London broil
3 Tbs. soy sauce
2 Tbs. mirin
1 Tbs. grated ginger
4 scallions, sliced in thin strips
½ cup flour
½ cup peanut oil
Lemon wedges for garnish

Flatten the meat until it is ¼″ thick, then cut into 3″ × 4″ slices. In a large bowl thoroughly mix the soy sauce, mirin and ginger. Marinate the meat in this mixture for 1 hour, turning often.

Remove meat from marinade, place some scallion strips on each slice, and roll tightly. Flour the rolls and seal them with moistened flour.

Fry a few rolls at a time in well-heated peanut oil, turning often to brown, about 3 minutes on each side. Drain, arrange on a platter and garnish with lemon wedges.

Serves 4

MEATBALLS IN SWEET AND SOUR SAUCE

1 lb. ground beef
1 large onion, minced
1 Tbs. cornstarch
mixed with 1 Tbs. dashi
1 Tbs. vegetable oil
2 scallions (whites and a little green), minced, for garnish

Sweet and Sour Sauce:
1 cup dashi
1 Tbs. soy sauce
1 Tbs. wine vinegar
1 Tbs. sugar
1 Tbs. cornstarch
¼ tsp. salt

Thoroughly combine the meat and onion with the cornstarch mixture. Form into meatballs the size of small golf balls. Brown meatballs in the oil, cover and cook for 5 minutes.

To make the sauce, combine the dashi, soy sauce, vinegar and sugar in a saucepan. Stir, bring to a simmer and cook for 3 minutes. Thicken with the cornstarch, then add salt.

Arrange the meatballs on dinner plates, spoon the sauce over them and garnish with scallions.

Serves 2-3

SPICY BEEF

2 lbs. flank steak, shredded
4 Tbs. sweet sherry
½ cup soy sauce
1 Tbs. sugar
¾ cup vegetable oil
8 dried chili peppers
2 celery stalks, shredded
1 carrot, peeled and thinly sliced
Salt to taste
2 Tbs. sesame oil
1 tsp. crushed peppercorns

Marinate the steak in the sherry, soy sauce and sugar for at least ½ hour, turning often. In a wok heat half the oil, add meat and keep turning for 5 minutes or until oil is absorbed. Remove meat to a dish and reserve.

Add the rest of the oil to the wok and heat the peppers until dark in color, turning often. Add celery and carrots, stir, add salt and cook over a medium flame for 3 minutes.

Return beef to wok and stir-fry for 1 minute. Sprinkle with sesame oil and peppercorns, turn and place in a hot serving bowl.

Serves 4

BEEF WITH ONIONS

2 Tbs. soy sauce
1 tsp. sugar
2 Tbs. cornstarch
3 Tbs. sesame oil
2 lbs. flank steak, thinly sliced
¼ cup vegetable oil
3 large onions, thinly sliced
1 tsp. salt
2 cloves garlic, minced

Sauce:
3 Tbs. soy sauce
2 Tbs. sherry
2 Tbs. sugar
2 Tbs. cornstarch dissolved in ½ cup water

In a large mixing bowl combine the soy sauce, sugar and cornstarch. Add the sesame oil and blend until smooth. Add the sliced meat and toss well. Place in refrigerator for 30 minutes, turning several times during chilling.

While the meat is chilling, combine the sauce ingredients, stir well and reserve to cook later.

Heat half the vegetable oil in a wok or heavy skillet. Add the onions and stir while cooking until lightly golden. Add salt, stir, and remove onions to a platter.

Add the balance of the vegetable oil to the wok, heat, add garlic and stir. Then add the meat and stir quickly for 1 minute. Add the onions, turning the mixture to blend.

Remove the meat and onions to a serving dish. Add the blended sauce to the wok and cook quickly, stirring. Turn into a sauce bowl and serve with the hot meat and onions.

Serves 4

TOMATO BEEF

2 lbs. sirloin steak
3 Tbs. cornstarch blended with 3 Tbs. water
2 Tbs. soy sauce
2 Tbs. sherry
½ cup peanut oil
1 onion, chopped
1 celery stalk, chopped
½ cup chopped green pepper
½ cup chopped red pepper
3 tomatoes, cut into chunks
½ cup sliced water chestnuts
1½ cups chicken broth
3 Tbs. chili sauce
1 Tbs. brown sugar
2 Tbs. brandy

Divide the steak into 4 equal parts. Mix the blended cornstarch, soy sauce and sherry and marinate the steak for 30 minutes, turning often.

Heat the oil in a large skillet and fry the steak, turning to sear and brown both sides. Remove to a heated platter.

Add the onions, celery, peppers, tomatoes and water chestnuts to the hot oil in the skillet and cook for 2 minutes, stirring all the time. Add the broth, stir, cover skillet and cook for 2 minutes.

Remove cover and stir in chili sauce, brown sugar and brandy. Increase heat, stir well and cook until mixture thickens.

Serve the steak and vegetables over a bed of rice with sauce from the skillet.

Serves 4

BEEF AND NOODLES

2 Tbs. sesame oil
2 lbs. beef, cut into 1½" cubes
¼ tsp. salt
⅛ tsp. white pepper
1 onion, chopped
2 cloves garlic, minced
½ tsp. ground nutmeg
3 whole cloves
3 Tbs. soy sauce
½ tsp. cumin
½ tsp. ground coriander
1 cup water
½ lb. Chinese cellophane noodles
or regular thin noodles

Heat the oil in a skillet and add the beef. Salt and pepper the meat while browning. Turn the meat a few times. Add all the remaining ingredients except the water and noodles.

When the meat is browned and the onions are still light-colored, add the cup of water and bring to a boil, stirring. Cover skillet, reduce heat and cook for 1½ hours.

Boil the noodles in salted water until tender. Rinse under hot water, drain, and serve covered with meat and sauce.

Serves 4-6

FRIED BEEF

¼ tsp. salt
⅛ tsp. freshly ground black pepper
1 tsp. turmeric
2 cloves garlic, crushed
1 onion, thinly sliced
2 lbs. beef, cut into slices ¼″ thick
1 cup vegetable oil for frying

In a large bowl toss together the seasonings, garlic and onion until thoroughly mixed. Add the beef slices and rub them all over with the mixture. Set aside to marinate for 1 hour.

Heat the oil in a large, heavy skillet. Add the meat and deep-fry, pressing it down to brown and crisp it. Remove to paper toweling to drain. Serve hot.

Serves 4

GINGER BEEF WITH TOMATOES

4 onions, finely minced
3 cloves garlic, minced
1 tsp. turmeric
½ tsp. ground chili pepper
1½ tsp. ground ginger
1 tsp. salt
2 lbs. lean beef, cut into 2″ cubes
3 Tbs. safflower oil
1½ cups beef bouillon
6 tomatoes, chopped

In a large wooden bowl pound together the onions, garlic, turmeric, chili pepper, ginger and salt. Rub this mixture all over the meat and allow to marinate in the bowl for 3 hours. Rub the meat again with the mixture every hour during marination.

Heat the oil, add the seasoned meat, pour in the bouillon and bring to a boil. Add the tomatoes, cover and lower heat to a simmer. Cook slowly for 1 hour or until meat is tender. Serve meat and sauce over a bed of rice.

Serves 4-6

BEEF AND TOMATOES

1 lb. sirloin steak, ¼" thick
2 Tbs. cornstarch blended
with 2 Tbs. soy sauce
3 Tbs. safflower oil
1 onion, chopped
2 tomatoes,
cut into small chunks
1 green pepper,
cut into large chunks
2 Tbs. sugar
Salt to taste
¾ cup chicken broth
1 Tbs. cornstarch mixed with
3 Tbs. warm water

Soak the steak in the cornstarch-soy mixture for 30 minutes. Heat the oil in a frying pan and stir-fry the steak until light brown on both sides. Remove to a heated platter.

Put the onions, tomatoes, green pepper, sugar and salt in the same pan and sauté for 5 minutes, stirring. Add the chicken broth and the cornstarch-water mixture. Blend well and cook at a slow simmer for 3 minutes. Stir.

Serve hot over rice.

Serves 2

LAMB DUMPLINGS

1 cup butter
2 lbs. leg of lamb, cut into ¼″ cubes
3 onions, sliced
1 tsp. crushed coriander
½ tsp. ground chili pepper
1 Tbs. turmeric
2 cloves garlic, minced
1 eggplant, peeled, sliced and mashed
4 cardamom seeds
8 dumplings (see p. 24 or use your own recipe)
1 cup water
2 cups plain yogurt
Salt and pepper to taste

Melt 4 Tbs. of the butter in a skillet. Add the meat, then the onions, coriander, chili pepper, turmeric and half the garlic. Stir and fry until meat browns and onions are lightly golden.

Add remainder of butter to the skillet and stir in the eggplant. Add cardamom seeds and stir. Drain the meat mixture and reserve.

Flatten the dumplings to form 4″ × 4″ squares. Place some of the meat mixture in the center of each dumpling and fold over opposite corners to form triangles. Press sides together to seal.

Boil the water, stir in the yogurt and the rest of the garlic, and add salt and pepper. Stir, add the dumplings and cook for 15 minutes. Remove dumplings to serving dishes with a slotted spoon and serve hot.

Serves 4

SAVORY LAMB

½ tsp. ground chili pepper
1 tsp. cumin
1/3 tsp. saffron
2 cloves garlic, minced
1 tsp. ground ginger
1 tsp. salt
¾ cup vinegar
¼ cup sesame oil
2 lbs. lean lamb,
 cut into ¾″ cubes
1 Tbs. lemon juice
Vegetable oil for cooking
½ cup chicken broth

In a large mixing bowl thoroughly blend the chili pepper, cumin, saffron, garlic, ginger, salt, vinegar and sesame oil. Add the lamb cubes and stir to saturate well. Add the lemon juice. Cover the bowl with plastic wrap or a cloth and marinate the lamb for an hour or longer, turning and stirring every 30 minutes.

Remove lamb to a heavy skillet and cook in hot oil, browning all over. When browned and half cooked, add chicken broth. Cook at a simmer for 35-40 minutes until meat is tender. Serve hot with noodles or rice.

Serves 4

ROAST LAMB

3 lbs. leg or shoulder of lamb, boned and cubed

½ cup sliced chutney as condiment

Marinade:

1 large onion, minced
1 celery stalk, minced
¼ cup white wine vinegar
1 Tbs. soy sauce
½ cup honey
3 Tbs. curry powder
½ tsp. coriander
¼ tsp. crushed red pepper
¼ tsp. salt
1 Tbs. grated lemon rind
Juice of 1 lemon

Mix all the marinade ingredients thoroughly. Add the lamb meat, soak thoroughly in the marinade, cover the bowl and place in refrigerator for 2 hours. Stir and mix well several times during marination.

Preheat oven to 400°.

Remove meat from refrigerator, drain off marinade and reserve. Put meat in a baking pan and bake for at least 30 minutes. Turn once and brush with marinade. Broil for the last 5 minutes until crispy.

Heat the reserved marinade and pour into a sauce bowl. Serve meat hot, accompanied by sauce and sliced chutney.

Serves 4-6

CHICKEN WITH ORANGE SOY SAUCE

1 lb. Japanese white radish, grated
1 cup orange juice
¾ cup soy sauce
¼ tsp. grated orange rind
1 2½-3-lb. soup chicken
3 qts. water
1 head Chinese cabbage, sliced
½ lb. fresh white mushrooms, sliced
¼ cup sake
1 Tbs. sugar
4 scallions, chopped

In a mixing bowl, combine thoroughly ¼ cup of the grated radish with the orange juice, soy sauce and grated orange rind. Reserve.

Cut up the chicken giblets, neck and back, add to the water in a large pot, and simmer for about 1½ hours. Strain off the stock and reserve. Discard the chicken parts.

Cut the chicken into small pieces, leaving skin and bones. In a large saucepan add the chicken pieces to the strained stock and cover tightly. Simmer for 1 hour until chicken is tender, skimming the fat off the top frequently. Add the remaining grated radish and the cabbage and mushrooms during the last 15 minutes of cooking.

Combine the reserved orange mixture with the sake and sugar and beat with a wooden spoon to dissolve sugar. Pour into dipping dishes and serve as a sauce.

Serve the chopped scallions in separate dishes and allow guests to help themselves to the chicken-vegetable soup.

Serves 4

CHICKEN IN MILK SAUCE

4 chicken breasts, skinned, boned and cut into thin strips
1 tsp. ginger juice
1 egg white, lightly beaten
A few Tbs. cornstarch
Vegetable oil for frying
1 lb. small mushrooms, stems trimmed, sliced thin
1 cup thinly sliced bamboo shoots
4 small slices of ham, cut into thin strips
½ cup chicken broth
¾ cup milk
1 tsp. cornstarch mixed with 1 tsp. water

Toss chicken strips with ginger juice. Dip each strip into egg white, dust with cornstarch and fry in 1″ of hot oil until lightly browned all over. Remove chicken to a wire rack to drain, and keep warm.

Sauté the mushrooms, bamboo shoots and ham in a little more oil, turning and mixing for about 3 minutes. Add chicken broth and milk and stir at a simmer for 2 minutes. Do not boil.

Stir in the cornstarch mixture to thicken. Add chicken strips, cook for 1 minute, and serve at once.

Serves 4

BAKED CHICKEN WITH MUSHROOMS AND CHEESE

3 chicken breasts, skinned, boned and thickly sliced
Salt to taste
2 Tbs. butter
¼ lb. fresh mushrooms, sliced
1 large sweet potato, peeled and sliced into long strips
1/3 cup grated Cheddar cheese
Lemon wedges for garnish

Preheat oven to 300°.

Sprinkle the chicken with a little salt. Lay out 4 8" squares of aluminum foil and cover each with a sheet of wax paper the same size.

Lightly butter the wax paper and divide the chicken slices, mushrooms, sweet potatoes and grated cheese equally onto the wax paper squares.

Fold excess wax paper over the ingredients and wrap tightly in foil. Bake the packages for 15 minutes and serve with a wedge of lemon.

Serves 4

CHICKEN IN A BAG

1 roasting chicken,
  cut into pieces
¼ cup slivered ginger
1 onion, sliced
3 carrots, sliced lengthwise
6 scallions, sliced in strips
½ lb. fresh mushrooms
3 medium-size potatoes,
  peeled and quartered
¼ cup chicken broth
¼ cup soy sauce

Preheat oven to 325°.

Make a bag out of aluminum foil and fill with all the ingredients. Be sure to secure the bag so that it holds the liquid. Bake for 50–60 minutes.

Heat a large serving bowl and empty into it contents of bag. Serve with buckwheat noodles.

Serves 4-6

ORANGE-GLAZED CHICKEN BALLS

½ lb. raw ground chicken
2 Tbs. breadcrumbs
1 egg, lightly beaten
1 tsp. soy sauce
1¼ cups boiling water
1 Tbs. sugar
1 Tbs. sweet soy sauce
1 cup orange juice
¼ cup grated orange rind

In a mortar pound the ground chicken with a pestle until light and fluffy. Add breadcrumbs, egg and soy sauce and mix well. Form mixture into balls 1″ in diameter.

Drop chicken balls into boiling water. Lower heat to a simmer and cook for 3 minutes. Add sugar, stir and add sweet soy sauce. Cover saucepan and cook slowly for 5 minutes. Add orange juice and orange rind.

Remove cover and raise heat. Stir and cook until liquid has evaporated, about 5 more minutes. Serve with rice and green vegetables.

Serves 2-3

CHICKEN STEAMED WITH KIRIN BEER

3 chicken breasts
3 Tbs. mirin
1 Tbs. soy sauce
Salt to taste
1 bottle of Kirin beer
1 scallion (white and 3″ of green), chopped
1 small onion, sliced
1″ cube of fresh ginger
1 cucumber, peeled, sliced into strips and chilled, with seedy portion removed, for garnish
2 tsp. dry mustard mixed into a paste with 2 tsp. hot water

Bone chicken breasts but leave skins on. Prick with a sharp knife.

Combine mirin, soy sauce and salt in a mixing bowl. Blend, add chicken and marinate for 30 minutes, turning every 10 minutes to saturate well.

Pour the beer into a large saucepan and add chicken and marinade. Stir, bring to a boil and cover. Steam for 10 minutes. Add scallions, onion and ginger and replace cover. Steam for 15 minutes more.

Remove chicken and take off skin. Slice chicken into 2½″-long strips and place in bowls. Garnish with cucumber strips and serve hot or at room temperature.

Blend mustard paste with 2 tsp. of sauce from the chicken pot and serve in small dishes for dipping. Pour remainder of sauce from pot into small dishes for dipping.

Serves 4-5

CHICKEN WITH NOODLES

3 cups milk
1 cup grated coconut
¼ cup vegetable oil
2 large onions, minced
4 cloves garlic, minced
1 tsp. chopped ginger
1 tsp. curry powder
1 4–5-lb. chicken, skinned, boned and cubed
¼ cup boiling water
1 tsp. salt
⅛ cup cornstarch mixed with ⅛ cup lukewarm water
¾ lb. broad noodles, cooked in salted water
1/3 tsp. ground chili pepper
3 hard-boiled eggs, chopped, for garnish
5 scallion whites, sliced, for garnish

Bring milk and coconut to a boil, remove from stove and let stand for ½ hour. Remove grated coconut with a slotted spoon, squeeze the juice into the milk, and discard coconut pulp. Reserve milk.

Heat the oil in a heavy skillet and saute the onions, garlic and ginger for about 8 minutes. Add curry and stir. Add chicken and cook for 20 minutes, stirring frequently.

Add ½ cup of the reserved coconut milk and stir. Add the boiling water and salt, stir, cover and cook for 10 minutes. Add the rest of the coconut milk and stir in the cornstarch mixture to thicken.

Place the noodles in large soup bowls and top with the chicken and sauce. Sprinkle each serving with ground chili pepper and garnish with chopped egg and scallions.

Serves 6–8

CHICKEN IN THE PAN

1 3-4-lb. chicken
½ tsp. ground chili pepper
¼ tsp. powdered ginger
8 Tbs. butter
¼ lb. raw rice
½ cup chopped green pepper
2 tomatoes, minced
1 cup thickly sliced fresh mushrooms
1 tsp. salt
3 onions, sliced
½ tsp. cumin
1 tsp. turmeric
3 tsp. coriander

Clean the chicken and pat the outside and the cavity dry with paper toweling. Rub inside and out with chili pepper and ginger.

Melt 4 Tbs. of the butter and mix with the rice. Add the green peppers, tomatoes, mushrooms and salt. Mix well and fill the chicken cavity with the rice stuffing.

Preheat oven to 325°.

Brown the onions in the remaining butter with the cumin, turmeric and coriander. Add the chicken and brown on all sides.

Remove the chicken and the browned onions to a baking pan with a cover. Add a little hot water and an extra dash of turmeric and salt. Cover the pan and bake for 1½ hours or until tender. If necessary add ½ cup hot water to gravy during baking.

Remove cover 10 minutes before chicken is done and increase heat to 400° so that chicken browns.

Serves 4

CHICKEN WITH PINEAPPLE AND WINE

3 Tbs. peanut oil
2 lbs. chicken white meat, cut into ½″ × ¼″ × 1½″ pieces
1 small can pineapple chunks, drained
1 cup sliced water chestnuts
1 large green pepper, chopped
1 medium-size onion, sliced
1 cup bamboo shoots
1 cup sliced bok choy
1¼ cups sliced celery
1 tsp. salt
¼ cup white wine vinegar
1 cup plum wine
1 cup pineapple juice
¾ cup sugar
2 kumquats, thinly sliced
2 Tbs. cornstarch dissolved in 2 Tbs. water
1 tsp. soy sauce

Heat a large skillet or wok, add the oil and stir-fry the chicken for 15–30 seconds. Add the pineapple and all the vegetables. Stir-fry for 5 seconds, add salt, stir and turn.

In a small bowl blend the vinegar, plum wine, pineapple juice, sugar and kumquats. Add to the chicken mixture and stir. Bring to a boil, cover and steam for 1½ minutes. Add cornstarch and stir. As the mixture thickens, add soy sauce.

Place the mixture in a large serving bowl and serve with noodles or rice.

Serves 6

CANTONESE CHICKEN

3 Tbs. peanut oil
2 chicken breasts, skinned, boned and sliced into strips
¼ lb. snow peas, trimmed and cut in half
1 celery stalk, thinly sliced
¼ lb. mushrooms, sliced
1 cup shredded bok choy
2/3 cup sliced water chestnuts
¼ cup chopped onion
2 tsp. soy sauce
3 cups chicken broth
1½ Tbs. cornstarch mixed with ½ Tbs. cold water

Heat the oil in a skillet and stir-fry the chicken strips for 2 minutes. Add the vegetables and soy sauce, and stir-fry for 2 minutes longer. Add the chicken broth and bring to a boil. Stir, cover, lower the heat and cook for 3 minutes. Remove cover and add cornstarch mixture, stirring until slightly thickened.

Place chicken and sauce in a deep bowl and serve hot, with rice on the side.

Serves 4

CHINESE ROAST CHICKEN

4 scallion whites, thinly sliced
1 tsp. ground ginger
2 Tbs. sherry
4 Tbs. soy sauce
2 Tbs. Worcestershire sauce
½ cup hoisin sauce
2 Tbs. brown sugar
4 Tbs. catsup
¼ tsp. dry mustard
1 roasting chicken
Chopped scallion greens for garnish

In a large bowl combine all the ingredients except the chicken and scallion greens. Mix well. Add chicken and allow to marinate for 2 hours, turning often to cover thoroughly inside and out.

Place chicken in a roasting pan and roast for 1¼ hours or longer, until brown and done. Cut into serving pieces with a cleaver.

Heat the marinade in a saucepan and pour over chicken when hot. Serve garnished with scallion greens, accompanied by rice and vegetables.

Serves 4

TANDOORI CHICKEN

1 3½-lb. chicken, whole
½ papaya, peeled and seeded
1 Tbs. finely chopped ginger
2 cloves garlic, finely chopped
1¾ Tbs. chopped chili peppers or chili powder
1 tsp. cumin
1 tsp. salt
Juice of 1 lemon
1 cup plain yogurt
1¾ Tbs. peanut oil
2 Tbs. melted butter or cooking oil

Thoroughly wash the chicken inside and out.

Mash the papaya, ginger, garlic, chili pepper, cumin and salt to form a smooth paste. Blend in lemon juice, yogurt and peanut oil.

Rub the chicken inside and out with the paste until all the paste is used up. Allow chicken to marinate for 1 hour.

Preheat oven to 375°. Skewer chicken on a rotisserie and roast for 1 hour, basting with butter or oil every 10 minutes. When chicken is browned and tender, serve hot with vegetables.

Serves 4

CHICKEN WITH SHRIMP AND RICE

1 large roasting chicken
1 leek, sliced
1 onion, sliced
3 sprigs of parsley
½ tsp. salt
⅛ tsp. black pepper
5½ cups water
1½ cups rice, washed
3 large onions, thinly sliced
3 cloves garlic, chopped
5 Tbs. cooking oil
½ lb. shrimp, shelled, cleaned and cooked
6 oz. crab meat, flaked
½ lb. cooked ham, cubed
1/3 tsp. each cumin, crushed coriander, crushed chili peppers and mace
1/3 cup peanut butter

Place the chicken, leek, onion, parsley, salt and pepper in a large soup pot with 5 cups of the water. Cook, covered, for 1½ hours until chicken is tender.

Remove chicken, drain and allow to cool. Slice chicken and discard bones. Reserve soup stock.

Put rice in a pot with the remaining ½ cup water and ½ cup of the soup stock. Salt and cook, covered, until rice is tender.

In a large skillet sauté the 3 sliced onions and the garlic in the oil until golden. Add cooked rice, brown and stir. Add sliced chicken, shrimp, crab meat, ham, seasonings and peanut butter. Stir to blend, then simmer for 9 minutes, stirring.

Serves 4-6

CHICKEN WRAPS

1 Tbs. butter or safflower oil
3 onions, minced
1 tsp. turmeric
¼ tsp. chopped chili peppers
2 tsp. ground coriander
4 cloves, crushed
¼ tsp. dry mustard
2 dashes of cinnamon
1 clove garlic, minced
Ground meat of 2 chickens
¼ cup chicken broth
4 potatoes, boiled and mashed
2 eggs beaten with 2 Tbs. milk
Breadcrumbs for dredging
Butter for frying
1 Tbs. lemon juice for garnish
¼ cup chopped parsley
for garnish

Heat the butter or oil in a large, heavy skillet. Add the onions, all the seasonings and the garlic. Stir and brown the onions. Add chicken, mix well and cook for about 2 minutes at a slow simmer.

Add chicken broth and cook for 10 minutes or until chicken is tender and done. Stir to mix well. Remove chicken mixture to a heated platter with a slotted spoon, allowing liquid to drain off.

Flatten a heaping Tbs. of mashed potato, place some of the chicken mixture in the center, fold over and form a potato ball. Flatten the ball into a ¼″-thick round. Repeat until you have used up the mashed potato and the chicken mixture.

Dip the rounds into the beaten egg mixture, then dredge in breadcrumbs. Fry in a little butter over low-to-moderate heat until browned on both sides. Remove to a heated serving platter, garnished with a sprinkling of lemon juice and chopped parsley. Serve with rice, fresh green peas and a spicy sauce.

Serves 6-8

SAUCY CHICKEN

½ cup peanut oil
3 cloves garlic, chopped
2 onions, minced
1 large chicken, cut into serving portions
1 green pepper, minced
1 red pepper, minced
¼ tsp. coriander
¼ tsp. salt
⅛ tsp. white pepper
1 Tbs. flour mixed into a paste with ½ cup white wine vinegar and 2½ Tbs. sugar
¼ cup water
4 tsp. soy sauce
Salt and pepper to taste
4 tomatoes, quartered
Chopped parsley for garnish

Heat the oil in a large, heavy skillet. Add the garlic and onions, stir, then add the chicken pieces and brown all over. Cover skillet and cook for 30 minutes.

Add the peppers, coriander, salt and pepper. Stir in the flour paste and add the water, soy sauce and salt and pepper to taste. Add tomatoes and stir.

Cover skillet and cook slowly for 30 minutes more until chicken is tender, stirring frequently. Serve chicken and sauce over a bed of rice, garnished with chopped parsley.

Serves 4

CHICKEN WITH LIVERS AND SHRIMP

¼ cup safflower oil
1 chicken breast, boned and sliced
1 lb. shrimp, shelled, cleaned and split
8 chicken livers
1 onion, sliced
1 clove garlic, minced
1 celery stalk, thinly sliced
¾ lb. thin noodles cooked in 2 cups chicken broth
1 Tbs. chopped ginger
2 Tbs. soy sauce
Salt and pepper to taste
1 Tbs. honey
2 tomatoes, cubed
2 Tbs. flour mixed with 3 Tbs. warm water

Heat the oil in a large skillet until very hot. Sauté the chicken, shrimp and livers for about 3 minutes, stirring and turning. Add the onion, garlic and celery and cook for 1 minute more, stirring.

Add the noodles and chicken broth, ginger, soy sauce, salt and pepper, honey, tomatoes and flour-water mixture. Cook for 5 minutes at a simmer, stirring to thicken. Serve hot in individual bowls.

Serves 4

8
Vegetables and Salads

The Japanese people were once vegetarians, and during the Zen Buddhist period they abstained from eating meat, poultry and fish. Over the past hundred years and more, their diet has changed, but their love of vegetables has never changed. The Japanese still enjoy vegetables, and now they eat them along with meat, chicken and fish.

Vegetables and salads, raw or cooked, are a part of most Japanese meals, including breakfast. When they are not the main course, they are served on the side in large bowls, raw, cooked or tempura-style (see Chapter 5, "Japanese Specialties," for tempura vegetables).

However they serve their vegetables, the Japanese emphasize proper cutting and slicing, both for eye appeal and to facilitate handling with chopsticks. The Japanese never overcook their vegetables; they like them just tender enough to eat but never soft or overdone.

Many vegetable dishes are served with sauces. The basic sauce ingredients are soy sauce, sherry and sake, but there are infinite combinations of these and other ingredients. Experiment with your own variations or consult the many sauce recipes that accompany the dishes in other chapters.

Vegetable Preparation

To the Japanese, the color, design and arrangement of vegetables are essential; they provide the elements for a display of the cook's artistic abilities. This section outlines the basics of vegetable preparation, but your vegetable carvings can be as elaborate as you wish. The more intricate the design, the more attractive the table, and the more successful the meal. The decorative possibilities are as limitless as your imagination.

Carrots, radishes, parsnips and lotus root can be cut into rings ¼″–½″ thick, or they can be cut into ½″–1″ cubes, as can cucumbers, potatoes and onions.

Cucumbers can also be sliced into rings, with or without the seedy center portions. If you remove the centers, you can stuff the rings with a paste made of mashed vegetable, cornstarch, dashi and soy sauce; spinach, carrots or peas make particularly good stuffings and create attractive displays.

Scallions, greens as well as whites, can be cut lengthwise into thin strips about 1½″ long.

Stringbeans can be sliced diagonally into 1½″-long pieces.

Japanese radish, white radish, turnips and onions can be sliced into ½″ ovals or squares.

Ginger root can be peeled and shredded into 1″-long strips.

Roots, potatoes, carrots and all other firm vegetables can be sliced into rectangular strips.

Diced vegetables, cooked or uncooked, can be very attractive. Try tomatoes, green and red peppers, stringbeans, snow peas, radishes and dried mushrooms.

Winter melon can be thinly sliced into 1″-long rectangles.

Ginger, parsley, flat parsley, onions, leeks, scallions and many other roots and vegetables can be finely chopped.

Salad Preparation

Japanese salads and salad dressings are more complex and varied than those Americans enjoy, and in Japanese cuisine it is very important to serve the right dressing with a particular salad. There are two basic salad styles: *aemono,* composed of cooked foods, and *sunomono,* composed of raw fish, seafood and vegetables tossed with various vinegar dressings.

Concoct your own imaginative salad combinations and then select a dressing that is appropriate to the ingredients you've chosen. You and your guests will be delighted with the results.

AEMONO DRESSINGS
For Salads Made with Cooked Mixed Vegetables or Cooked Foods Combined with Vegetables

Goma-aemono: Mix ¼ cup hot dashi thoroughly with ¼ cup toasted sesame seeds, chopped or ground, 2 Tbs. soy sauce and 2 Tbs. sugar. This dressing is excellent with cooked green vegetables. For a variation, substitute ¼ cup crushed walnuts for the sesame seeds.

Karashi-aemono: Mix 1 tsp. hot Japanese mustard into a paste with 1 tsp. dashi. Blend in 1 Tbs. soy sauce and 1½ Tbs. dashi. A good dressing for cooked vegetables accompanying pork or chicken dishes.

Wasabi-aemono: Mix 1 tsp. prepared Japanese horseradish with 3 Tbs. soy sauce. A fine dressing for fish and vegetables.

Oil and vinegar: Combine 3 Tbs. sesame oil, 1 Tbs. soy sauce and ½ Tbs. rice vinegar. Shake well. A basic dressing that goes well with almost any cooked salad.

SUNOMONO DRESSINGS
For Salads Made of Raw Fish, Shellfish and Vegetables (Also Fine for Cooked Salads)

Sambai-zu: Thoroughly combine 2½ Tbs. rice vinegar, 2½ Tbs. dashi, ¼ cup sugar, 2 tsp. soy sauce and ⅛ tsp. salt. This seafood and vegetable dressing also makes a good dipping sauce.

Pon-zu: Mix 5 Tbs. lemon juice with 5 Tbs. soy sauce. A good, simple seafood dressing.

Ama-zu: Combine ¼ cup rice vinegar, 2 Tbs. soy sauce, ⅛ cup sugar, 1 Tbs. cornstarch, ¼ cup water and a dash of sesame oil. Bring to a boil, stirring constantly. A good, thick dressing for raw fish and vegetables.

Kurumi-zu: Thoroughly mix ¼ cup finely chopped walnuts, 1 Tbs. sugar, 3 Tbs. rice vinegar, 2 Tbs. soy sauce and a pinch of salt. Good with any dish.

Karashi-zu: Combine 1 Tbs. Japanese mustard or hot English mustard with 1 egg yolk, lightly beaten, 1 Tbs. rice vinegar and 1 tsp. sugar. Shake well. Good as a dressing for vegetables served with pork, beef and smoked meats.

9
Desserts

The people of Japan and Southeast Asia are not as fond of desserts as are the people of the Western world. Though their cuisine does feature a few desserts, the list is quite limited. However, if you want to include a Japanese-style dessert on your menu, you can do so by putting your imagination and culinary expertise to work.

For example, excite the palate with butter ginger cookies made of the usual ingredients—butter, eggs and flour—but spiced with fresh-squeezed ginger juice.

A fruit compote composed of pineapple, mandarin oranges, honey, bananas and grated coconut can be delightful with the addition of 1 or 2 Tbs. of orange liqueur.

Or you can take plain vanilla ice cream and give it a Japanese flavor by blending in grated ginger and walnuts—¼ tsp. ginger and 2 Tbs. walnuts per pint of ice cream. Top with more grated walnuts and a slice of brandied kumquat.

There are many more such possibilities for the creative cook once the recipes in this chapter are exhausted. And after all, creativity is the essence of the Japanese cuisine.

MANDARIN SNOW SPONGE

1 Tbs. vanilla gelatin
½ cup cold water
2 4-oz. cans of mandarin oranges
2 cups sugar
2 egg whites, stiffly beaten
½ tsp. vanilla extract

Soften the gelatin in the water. Add the liquid from the oranges and mix in the sugar. Cook at a simmer for 5 minutes, stirring. Allow to cool. Whip in the egg whites gently, then stir in the vanilla.

Pour into a bowl and cool in the refrigerator until almost set. Then press the mandarin oranges into the surface and return to the refrigerator to harden. Cut into small squares and serve.

Serves 4

BURMA DOUGHNUTS

2 cups sugar
1½ cups water
1 tsp. saffron
2½ Tbs. boiling water
1¼ cups flour, sifted
1 tsp. baking powder
Salt to taste
¼ cup vegetable oil for frying
Cinnamon or nutmeg or both to sprinkle

Cook the sugar and 1 cup of the water in a saucepan over moderate heat until a thick syrup forms. Stir often. Reserve.

Soak the saffron in the boiling water for 5 minutes. Meanwhile, sift the flour, baking powder and salt into a bowl. Add the remaining ½ cup water and the saffron mixture and blend into a smooth batter.

Pour the oil into a skillet and heat to 375°. Pour the batter into the oil in 2½" lengths, as many as will fit in the pan. Fry until golden, remove and drain in paper toweling. When cool, dip in the sugar-water syrup to cover all over. Sprinkle with cinnamon or nutmeg.

Serves 6-8

COCONUT CREAM

2 cups grated fresh coconut
2 cups milk
1¼ cups sugar
5 eggs, well beaten
Grated coconut for garnish

Put the coconut and milk into a saucepan, bring to a boil and remove from heat. Let the coconut soak for 15-20 minutes. Drain off the milk and reserve. Discard coconut meat.

Preheat oven to 350°.

Add the sugar to the beaten eggs and beat again until light and fluffy. Pour in the reserved milk and beat to blend.

Pour the custard into 8 buttered custard cups, filling each cup a little more than halfway. Cover the cups and place them in a large pan of water. Bake for 15-20 minutes until the custard sets. Allow to cool and place in refrigerator to chill. Remove, sprinkle with grated coconut and serve.

Serves 8

FRUIT CHUTNEY

¾ cup wine or cider vinegar
1 cup white sugar
1 cup brown sugar
¾ cup raisins
½ cup sliced ginger
¼ cup chopped onion
¼ lb. dried apples
¼ lb. dried apricots or peaches
2 cups pitted quartered prunes
2 Tbs. chopped lemon rind
¼ tsp. nutmeg
4 cloves, mashed
2 cloves garlic, minced
½ tsp. dry mustard
1 tsp. ground red pepper
Salt to taste

Bring the vinegar to a boil in a saucepan and slowly add the sugar, mixing until it dissolves. Gradually add all the remaining ingredients.

Cook slowly and stir often until the mixture thickens to the consistency of fruit preserves. This should take 15-20 minutes or less, but cook longer if necessary.

The chutney can be served as a dessert or as an accompaniment to the meal. It can also be stored in sterilized sealed jars and frozen or refrigerated for use as needed.

Makes 2 quarts

GLAZED APPLES

2 eggs, beaten
1 cup water
1 cup flour
6 crisp apples,
 cored and cut in eighths*
Vegetable oil for frying
Ice water

Glaze:
8 Tbs. peanut oil
9 Tbs. sugar
2 Tbs. honey

Combine the eggs, water and flour, stirring to make a very smooth batter. Dip the apple pieces in the batter and fry in deep oil a few at a time until browned, about 3–4 minutes. Drain on paper toweling.

To make the glaze, put the peanut oil in a saucepan and add the sugar and honey. Cook until a thick syrup forms. Dip the apple pieces quickly in the glaze and then dip immediately in ice water. Remove quickly and drain.

Serves 6

*You can substitute bananas for the apples.

FRIED SWEET POTATOES

2 lbs. sweet potatoes or yams
Peanut oil for frying
12 Tbs. corn syrup or honey
1 Tbs. water

Peel the sweet potatoes and cut them into slices about 2″ long and ½″ thick. Pat dry and fry in oil until golden brown and crisp, turning once. Drain and place on a warm platter.

Heat the syrup and water until blended and pour over the potatoes. Serve hot.

Serves 4

WHEATCAKES

3 cups wheat flour
1⅞ cups water, almost boiling
5 Tbs. cooking oil

Make a soft dough by mixing the flour and water. Roll out on a floured board until very thin. Cut out 24 rounds 2″ in diameter. Brush 12 of the rounds with oil, then place the other 12 rounds on top of them. Roll the layered rounds out until double in size.

Heat the remaining oil in a frying pan with a lid. Fry each round about 3 minutes on one side, covered, then repeat for the other side. Cover a serving dish with a clean white cloth, separate the layered wheatcakes and lay out on the dish.

Makes 24 wheatcakes

COCONUT PASTRIES

4 oz. shredded coconut
6 Tbs. white sugar
6 Tbs. brown sugar
1 Tbs. cornstarch
5 Tbs. water
1 unbaked 9″ pie crust
1 egg, beaten

Preheat oven to 400°.

In a saucepan add the coconut, white sugar, brown sugar and cornstarch to the water and bring to a boil. Stir until thick and well blended. Allow to cool.

Roll out the pie crust on a floured board until ⅛″ thick. With the top of a glass cut out 3″ circles. Place 1 tsp. of the coconut mixture in the center of each, fold over, brush the edges with egg and press with a fork to seal.

Place the pastries on a cookie sheet, brush the tops with egg, then prick. Bake for 15-20 minutes, until lightly browned. Cool and serve.

Makes 20 pastries

COCONUT RICE PUDDING

1 cup raw rice
3 cups water
½ tsp. salt
¾ cup sugar
1/3 cup grated coconut
1 cup milk
1 Tbs. grated lemon rind
1 tsp. nutmeg

Boil the rice in a saucepan with the water and salt. Cover and simmer for 15 minutes or until rice is tender and water is absorbed.

Add the sugar, coconut and milk. Mix well, lower the heat and cook until mixture is creamy, about 10 minutes. Stir in the lemon rind, sprinkle with nutmeg and serve cool.

Serves 4

CUSTARD SUPREME

2 cups grated coconut
2 cups cream
1 cup brown sugar
3 Tbs. water
4 eggs, beaten
2 egg yolks, beaten
1 cup white sugar
1 Tbs. grated lemon rind

Bring the coconut and cream almost to a boil. Remove from heat and let the coconut soak for ½ hour. Drain off the cream. Press the juice from the coconut meat and add it to the cream, discarding meat.

Heat the brown sugar and water in a saucepan, stirring until it becomes a thick syrup. Put ¾ of the syrup in a greased cake tin and mix the rest with the coconut cream. Cook the syrup-cream mixture over low heat, stirring until smooth and thick.

Combine the eggs, egg yolks, white sugar and lemon rind and beat well. Add the syrup-cream mixture slowly, beating it in. Pour into the cake tin with the syrup and place the tin in a pan of water. Cook over low heat, with the water just simmering, for 1¼ hours or until custard sets. Serve hot or cooled.

Serves 4

GINGER CAKE

2¼ cups flour
1 tsp. baking soda
1¼ tsp. baking powder
¼ tsp. salt
1 Tbs. ground ginger
¼ tsp. cinnamon
Dash of nutmeg
¾ cup sugar
¾ cup cooking oil
1 cup molasses
¾ cup boiling water
2 eggs, beaten

Preheat oven to 350°.

Sift together the flour, baking soda and powder, salt and spices. In a separate bowl combine the sugar, oil, molasses and boiling water. Blend with the flour mixture and fold in the beaten eggs.

Pour the cake batter into a square greased pan and bake for 35–40 minutes. Serve hot or cold.

Serves 6–8

APPLE CAKE

2/3 cup brown sugar
¼ tsp. each cinnamon, nutmeg coriander, ginger and salt
1 Tbs. grated lemon rind
1 tsp. lemon juice
1/3 cup melted butter
1 cup breadcrumbs
2½ cups peeled, cored, sliced green apples
1/3 cup water

Preheat oven to 350°.

Sift the sugar and spices into a bowl, then mix in the lemon rind and lemon juice.

Blend the butter and breadcrumbs and spread ¼ cup of the crumbs on the bottom of a buttered baking pan. Spread half the apples on top of the crumbs, then sprinkle with half the sugar mixture. Spread on another ½ cup of breadcrumbs, then the rest of the apples.

Pour the water into the pan gently and sprinkle with remaining breadcrumbs and sugar. Cover and bake for 35–40 minutes or until apples are tender. Remove cover and bake for another 10 minutes, until the top browns and most of the liquid is absorbed. Serve hot.

Serves 4

Glossary

The following ingredients, used extensively in Oriental cooking, are available in Oriental groceries, gourmet shops, specialty stores and many fine supermarkets.

Azuki beans: a Chinese vegetable also known as advuki beans. They come in a wide variety of colors.

Bean curd: a vegetable cheese made from pureed soybeans, treated and presssed. Bean curd has a custard consistency and is available in square cakes.

Bird's nest (edible): the nest of various small swifts of southern Asia, made chiefly of glutinous secretions of the salivary gland. Available in small packages, 4–8 oz.

Bonito: a medium-size fish also known as blue-stripe bonito, and known in Japanese markets as katsuobushi. Available fresh or dried and flaked.

Bok choy: a variety of Chinese cabbage that grows like celery, with long white stalks and dark green leaves.

Burdock root: the slender, long root of *Arctium lappa,* pared and used in simmered dishes.

Chinese mustard: available prepared, or mix equal parts of dried mustard and boiling water to make a thick paste, then let stand for 20 minutes.

Chinese spices: a prepared mixture of ground black pepper, cinnamon, fennel, anise, cloves and Chinese salt.

Chutney: a condiment made from ginger, garlic, sugar, mango slices or other fruits, vinegar and spices. Available prepared.

Daikon: a large white radish that keeps in the refrigerator for a couple of weeks.

Dashi: a soup stock made from seaweed (kelp) and dried bonito (see p. 35 for recipe). Dashi adds a subtle flavor to soups and can also be used to flavor other cooked foods.

Duck sauce: a Chinese sweet sauce, sold in jars or cans.

Ginger root: a knobby, pale, spicy vegetable root that keeps in the refigerator for several weeks. It can be grated, chopped, sliced or squeezed to obtain ginger juice.

Ginkgo nut: a meaty nut used in soups or roasted and chopped for use in sauces, salads and meat dishes. Available in cans.

Hoisin sauce: a sauce used in preparing wok dishes, seafood, chicken and pork. It adds a sweet and spicy pumpkin flavor.

Kamaboko: Japanese fish sausage in paste.

Mirin: a sweet rice wine used in cooking.

Miso: a paste made from cooked, fermented soybeans. There are two types, aka miso, made from red soybeans, and shiro miso, a white bean paste.

Mochigome: sweet rice.

Oriental 7 spices: a prepared spice consisting of sesame, mustard, poppyseed, pepper, sage and tangerine peel blended and powdered. Sold in jars and shake bottles.

Sake: a fermented rice wine served warm for drinking and used extensively in Japanese cooking.

Shirataki vermicelli: transparent noodles made from Oriental plants, then shredded. Available fresh or canned.

Taro root: the starchy, tuberous root of the taro plant, used to flavor soups and other dishes.

Wakame: large-leafed dried seaweed, used as a garnish.

Wondra flour: a very fine, well-sifted dusting flour, available in shaking containers.

Recipe Index

Country Index

Burma

China

Hong Kong

Indonesia

Japan

Thailand